NATIONAL
GEOGRAPHIC
KiDS

# kids
## vs. PLASTIC

**DITCH THE STRAW** AND FIND THE **POLLUTION SOLUTION** TO BOTTLES, BAGS, AND OTHER **SINGLE-USE PLASTICS**

HOW **YOU** CAN BE A **WASTE WARRIOR!**

**JULIE BEER**

NATIONAL GEOGRAPHIC
WASHINGTON, D.C.

# CONTENTS

## CHAPTER 5 — PLASTICS REPACKAGED 70

## CHAPTER 6 — THE END OF THE LINE: RECYCLE! 86

## CHAPTER 7 — LOOKING AHEAD 102

# A PLASTIC PLANET

## SOMETHING PRETTY PROFOUND IS HAPPENING TO OUR PLANET. IT'S BEING SWAMPED BY PLASTIC.

Humans have created about nine billion tons (8.2 billion t) of plastic over the past 70 years, and we create 448 million tons (406 million t) more every year. Today, more than a third of all new plastic is made for packaging that is mostly designed to be used once and then thrown away.

Although we can't control what everyone else in the world does, we can make choices in our own lives to reduce and improve how we use plastic. Then we can teach others about how plastic is affecting the environment and how they can help, too.

### The Problem With Plastic

Why is plastic such a big problem? Well, for starters, it takes a *realllly* long time to bio-degrade (or break down into tiny microscopic pieces). No one knows exactly how long it takes, but depending on the type of plastic, it could be 20 years, 600 years, or even more.

Plastic also contributes to climate change, which is mostly caused by the burning of fossil fuels like gas and coal. The effects of climate change include the overall warming of our planet, melting ice caps, rising sea levels (which can cause flooding), extreme weather (like heat waves and droughts), and more. And guess what we use to make plastic? Fossil fuels. A recent study found that as plastic degrades in the sun-light, it releases greenhouse gases, which trap heat in our atmosphere and contribute to cli-mate change as well.

Then there's all the plastic that's polluting our oceans and harming thousands—or poten-tially millions—of marine animals. Animals get tangled up in it. They eat it, mistaking it for floating bits of food. They're all literally swim-ming in plastic.

### A Place to Start

Plastic is just one piece of the global pollution crisis, but addressing this one issue is a great place to start in the overall cleanup of our planet. National Geographic's explorers and top scientists are using their expertise to identify the activities taking place on land, particularly near rivers, that contribute to the flow of plastic entering our oceans. Then they're using what they learn to inspire change at home and around the world. Numerous states and cities have restricted the use of single-use plastic—the kind you use once and then throw away, like plastic straws—and several states have banned single-use plastic bags.

### The Pollution Solution

National Geographic is working hard to gather the best in research, technology, education, and storytelling to create incredible change. But we can't do this without help. We need you.

You are a really important part of finding solutions to plastic pollution. Your actions, the choices you make, and your leadership at school and at home will make an immediate difference to your local environment. By working together, we can create change on a global scale and pro-tect our oceans and rivers and the precious, irreplaceable wildlife on land and in the sea.

We've arranged this book in the same order that you can approach your own plastic use: First, try to reduce your plastic consumption and avoid buying new plastic altogether. Next, find creative ways to reuse the plastic you already have, a practice called upcycling. Lastly, instead of sending plastic to the landfill, use the chart in this book to find out what you can recycle! Reduce, reuse, recycle ... Sound famil-iar? As you go through, you'll see a recurring "Take Action!" logo, which highlights concrete things you can do right now to be a waste warrior!

Excited to get started? Turn the page to become an environmental changemaker!

PLASTICWARE LIKE THESE PLATES, FORKS, AND CUPS HAVE BECOME COMMONPLACE—BUT THEY DON'T HAVE TO BE! CHECK OUT THE ECO-FRIENDLY ALTERNATIVE OPTIONS IN THIS CHAPTER.

# CHAPTER 1

# PLASTIC 101

>> **TAKE A LOOK AROUND. PLASTIC IS EVERYWHERE.** It's hard to imagine going a day without eating from, playing with, or even sitting on something made of plastic. We use millions of tons of it every year. So what's the big deal about plastic? Why is it so popular? And what exactly is it? Let's dive in to find out the answers to these questions, and then explore what happens to plastic once we're done with it. We'll even hear from one teen who questioned his own plastic use, which in turn has changed the way many of us slurp up our beverages today. Are you ready?

# IT ALL ADDS UP

Since 1950, humans have created a grand total of NINE BILLION TONS (8.2 billion t) of plastic. How does it measure up? NINE BILLION TONS IS EQUIVALENT TO THE WEIGHT OF...

**25,000**
EMPIRE STATE BUILDINGS

**360 MILLION**
GARBAGE TRUCKS

45 MILLION BLUE WHALES

1 BILLION ELEPHANTS

800,000 EIFFEL TOWERS

# WHAT IS PLASTIC?

**P**lastic can be molded, colored, and textured to make, well, just about anything. That begs the question, what precisely is this wonder product? Who invented it? How is it made? Let's find out.

## THE BASICS:
Plastics are polymers, or long, flexible chains of molecules made of repeating links. It's this molecular structure that makes plastic lightweight, hard to break, and easy to mold into just about any shape—all of which makes it extremely useful.

## WHERE DO POLYMERS COME FROM?
Polymers can be found in nature, in things like the cell walls of plants, tar, tortoiseshell, amber, and tree sap. In fact, nearly 3,500 years ago, people in what is today Central America used the sap from gum trees to make rubber balls for games. About 150 years ago, scientists first started replicating the polymers in nature to improve on them—these are called synthetic polymers.

## WHO INVENTED PLASTIC?
Synthetic types of plastic, the kind we're most familiar with, weren't invented until the 19th century. The first few types of plastic created weren't very bendable (or useful), but in 1869, an American named John Wesley Hyatt created the first practical synthetic polymer. At the time, the discovery was a big deal: For the first time, manufacturing was no longer limited by the resources supplied by nature, like wood, clay, and stone. People could create their own materials.

## WHAT IS SYNTHETIC PLASTIC MADE FROM?
Today, most plastic is made from oil and natural gas.

## WHEN DID IT BECOME POPULAR?
World War II was a big moment for plastic. Nylon, which is strong and light like silk, but made of plastic, was used for parachutes, rope, body armor, and helmet liners. Plastic glass, also known as Plexiglas, was (and still is) a lightweight, safer alternative to glass for airplane windows. After the war, plastic entered the mainstream. Everything from dishes to radios to Mr. Potato Head (a popular toy) hit the market. A few decades later, plastic soda bottles became a lightweight nonbreakable alternative to glass bottles, and grocery stores switched from paper bags to cheaper thin plastic ones.

## THAT BRINGS US TO TODAY.
Look around: Are you more than a few feet away from something plastic? Probably not! Plastic is all around us.

AMERICANS use an average of ONE plastic grocery bag A DAY. People in DENMARK use an average of FOUR plastic grocery bags PER YEAR.

# THE HISTORY OF PLASTIC

**1856:** British inventor creates an early (but not very functional) form of synthetic plastic.

**1869:** First commercially useful plastic made as a substitute for ivory, which is the tusks of elephants and marine mammals.

**1907:** Bakelite, a type of plastic that can easily be molded, is created, kick-starting the modern plastic era.

**1939:** Nylon stockings, or pantyhose, made of plastic fiber are introduced at the New York World's Fair.

**1939–1945:** Plastic becomes critical for the Allies during World War II for the production of parachutes, rope, and airplane windows.

**1949:** Earl Tupper patents Tupperware plastic bowls with sealing lids.

**1957:** Hula-Hoop fad creates a demand for polyethylene—a strong plastic used to make everything from milk jugs to shampoo bottles.

**1965:** Plastic shopping bags are invented.

**1978:** First plastic soda bottles are sold.

**1980:** Woodbury, New Jersey, is the first U.S. city to introduce curbside recycling.

**1997:** The Great Pacific Garbage Patch, a collection of plastic debris between Hawaii and California, is discovered.

**2009:** The United Nations calls for a global ban on plastic shopping bags.

**2014:** California becomes the first U.S. state to ban single-use plastic shopping bags.

**2016:** The Netherlands bans microbeads, tiny bits of plastic in products like body washes and scrubs.

**2018:** California full-service restaurants are banned from handing out straws unless customers request one.

**2019:** New York bans single-use plastic bags.

# GOING, GOING... NOT GONE

## ONCE IT'S TOSSED, PLASTIC STAYS AROUND.

>> **O**nly a small percentage of all the plastic that has ever been made has been recycled to make other things. Most has been tossed and left to slowly biodegrade in landfills, a process that can take hundreds of years. The other option to getting rid of plastic is to burn it. But because plastic is made from fossil fuels, that releases harmful pollutants into the air.

Here is a breakdown of where all the plastic has gone since people started making it, and if it does wind up in a landfill, how long it takes to biodegrade.

# WHERE DOES ALL THE PLASTIC GO?

**9%** Recycled

**12%** Burned, releasing toxins into the air

**79%** Sent to landfills or wound up in the natural environment (like oceans)

# THE LIFE SPAN OF PLASTIC

Plastic that's sent to a landfill doesn't just disappear—it stays there for a really long time. Different types of plastic take different lengths of time to biodegrade.

 **PLASTIC BAG**
**20 YEARS**

 **PLASTIC-FOAM CUP 50 YEARS**

 **STRAW**
**200 YEARS**

 **BOTTLE**
**450 YEARS**

 **SODA SIX-PACK RING 450 YEARS**

 **FISHING LINE**
**600+ YEARS**

# HOW PLASTIC GETS FROM LAND TO SEA

Every year, 8.8 million tons (8 million t) of plastic ends up in the world's oceans. That's the weight of 86 aircraft carriers! Researchers estimate that by 2050, the weight of all the plastic in the oceans will be greater than the weight of all the fish in the oceans. How does the plastic get there? It turns out, as the graphic shows, there are a number of different ways. For example, litter gets washed down storm drains. Trash is sometimes illegally dumped at beaches or near streams and rivers. Fishing gear can become marine trash when it is lost or abandoned.

Rain, wind, and strong storms can send trash (including plastic) into waterways that lead to the ocean. Some of the plastic in the ocean comes straight from our bathrooms! A recent study found that 20 percent of Americans who wear contact lenses flush them down the toilet when they're ready to dispose of them. These bits of plastic head down the drain and can wind up in the ocean. Another surprising plastic that travels from our bathrooms to the ocean? Microbeads. These tiny bits of plastic are found in some shower gels and face scrubs. They may make us squeaky clean, but they are plastic pollution for the ocean.

# Take Action!

## DON'T FLUSH THOSE LENSES.

**Remind your** contact lens–wearing family members to dispose of their contacts in the trash, not down the drain. Or even better: Ask your parents to look online for a contact lens recycling program.

More than **10 PERCENT OF THE PLASTIC** that ends up in the ocean reaches it via Asia's Yangtze River.

# THE LAST STRAW

## Q&A With Teen Anti-Straw Advocate Milo Cress

**W**hen Milo Cress was nine years old, he noticed that every time he ordered a drink at a restaurant in his hometown in Vermont, it automatically came with a straw. He didn't use his straw, so he took it out of the drink and set it aside. It couldn't be reused by someone else, so it was thrown away when the waitstaff cleared the table. He saw that a lot of straws were being thrown away, whether customers used them or not. Milo thought this was a big waste, which got him thinking: Just how many plastic straws are thrown away in the United States? He did a little investigating on the computer and couldn't find any good information. So he picked up the phone and did his own research. He called three major straw manufacturers in the United States and asked them to estimate the number of straws Americans use every day. The number he landed on was about 500 million—that's 1.5 straws per person per day! Milo got to work getting the word out and launched the "Be Straw Free" project. Now at age 19, Milo is a spokesperson for reducing plastic waste.

**Q: Your figure that Americans use 500 million straws a day launched a massive straw-free movement in the U.S. How did you spread that information?**
**Milo:** I first started talking to people about straws—individuals and restaurant owners. Then restaurants put up information tables about my work. Pretty soon, I met with the governor of Vermont, and I testified before the Vermont legislature. Then the media picked up on it.

**Q: You were just nine years old when you started your Be Straw Free project. Did you feel like you were being taken seriously?**
**Milo:** Yes! Not in spite of the fact that I was a kid, but because of it. Not many people my age were talking about this, so my

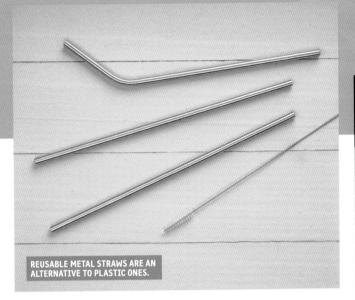

REUSABLE METAL STRAWS ARE AN ALTERNATIVE TO PLASTIC ONES.

SOME U.S. CITIES HAVE BANNED PLASTIC STRAWS FROM FULL-SERVICE RESTAURANTS.

voice stood out. Adults tend to think kids aren't interested in environmental, social justice, political, or economic issues, so when we do speak up about these topics, adults will often stop and listen.

### Q: Has it been hard to convince people to say no to straws?

**Milo:** Not really. Restaurants that I worked with that adopted the offer-first policy asked people if they wanted a straw instead of serving one automatically. The restaurants reported back to me that 50 to 80 percent of the time customers opted not to take the straw. Most people, it seems, had really just never given it a second thought.

### Q: Some restaurants have switched to alternative-material straws or stopped offering straws automatically. Do you think people are becoming more aware of the straw issue?

**Milo:** Yes. People have reached out to me and said, "I've stopped using straws. What other ways can I reduce my plastic use?" Environmental awareness leads to more environmental awareness.

### Q: What do you personally do to cut down on plastic?

**Milo:** I carry around a reusable straw. I use reusable bags instead of disposable ones. I drink from reusable bottles. I haven't used a plastic water bottle in several years!

## Take Action!

## WHAT'S THE ALTERNATIVE?

**Good news!** You don't have to give up drinking your smoothies and shakes with a straw. Try using a reusable plastic, metal, or glass one. There are even super-skinny scrub brushes to clean out the straws' nooks and crannies. Remind your parents to keep a few reusable straws in the car—and carry one in your backpack!—so you'll always be ready to say no to plastic when you're on the go.

# 480 BILLION

SINGLE-USE PLASTIC BOTTLES ARE SOLD **EVERY YEAR.** THAT'S NEARLY

# ONE MILLION

SOLD **EVERY MINUTE** ... OR **15,000 SOLD** EVERY SECOND. THAT'S AN AVERAGE OF **65 PLASTIC BOTTLES** FOR **EVERY PERSON** ON EARTH.

**LESS THAN 50 PERCENT** OF PLASTIC BOTTLES ARE COLLECTED FOR RECYCLING.

ONLY 7 PERCENT ARE TURNED INTO **NEW BOTTLES.**

## SINGLE-USE PLASTIC BOTTLES,

designed to be used once and then thrown away, are one of the most common types of plastic waste.

## IT TAKES 17 MILLION BARRELS OF OIL

to make all the plastic bottles Americans use each year. That's enough oil to keep a million cars going for 12 months!

## Take Action!

### HERE'S HOW YOU CAN PASS ON PLASTIC WATER BOTTLES.

**1** **Drink tap water.** As long as your drinking water is considered safe, grab a glass of water straight from the faucet.

**2** **Carry** a reusable bottle with you to school, sports games, and after-school activities.

**3** **Pack** an empty water bottle in your suitcase for trips so you can refill on the go.

**4** **Talk** to your principal about holding an assembly at school, encouraging students to go plastic bottle free!

**5** **Help** start a campaign for your school to install a water bottle refill station.

In the United Kingdom, every major city will have a WATER REFILL STATION by 2021.

## I Spy Plastic in the Bedroom

Got plastic? If you look closely, plastic is scattered all around your everyday life—more than you might realize. It's even hanging out in your bedroom! Test your plastic-spotting skills to see if you can find 16 common plastic items in this room. Then check the answer key to see how you did.

**Answers**

- Plastic toy train
- Portable stereo
- CDs
- Red plastic tub
- Butterfly twinkle lights
- Markers
- Clear plastic tub
- Striped pencil pouch
- Red marker case
- Plastic toy house
- Rainbow wastebasket
- Cup holding paintbrush
- Lamp cord
- Cow figure
- Microplastics in the clothes
- Acrylic yarn in plastic bag
- Plastic binder

A DOLPHIN IS ENTANGLED IN A PLASTIC SIX-PACK RING THAT MADE ITS WAY INTO THE OCEAN.

# CHAPTER 2

# AN OCEAN OF PLASTIC

**PLASTIC THAT WINDS UP IN WATERWAYS AND OCEANS ISN'T JUST TRASH,** it's a danger to the marine animals that live there—from birds that feed in these waters and live along shorelines to animals that swim in the water, like turtles, dolphins, seals, and fish. Animals get tangled in nets left by people fishing, they get caught up in plastic bags that drift in the water, and they eat plastic they mistakenly think is food. Luckily, scientists, inventors, and even kids are working on solutions for cleaning up plastic and keeping it from entering waterways. Want to learn more and find out what you can do to help? Read on!

# 8.8 MILLION TONS
(8 MILLION MT)
# OF PLASTIC
# IS DUMPED IN THE
# OCEAN
# EVERY YEAR.

Plastic has been found in the deepest parts of the ocean, up to **6.8 MILES (11 km) BELOW THE SURFACE.**

Scientists recently discovered that sea anemones are **EATING** tiny bits of microplastics along with their food.

**THAT'S ABOUT THE WEIGHT OF ...**

SCHOOL BUS

STOP

**533,000 SCHOOL BUSES**

**2,810 LONDON EYE FERRIS WHEELS**

**97 WASHINGTON MONUMENTS**

**THAT'S EQUAL TO ....**

**Five plastic grocery bags per every foot (0.3 m) of coastline around the globe**

**One garbage truck's worth of plastic dumped into the ocean every minute for a year.**

While *we* know that the plastic that finds its way into the world's oceans is trash, to the fish that live there, it looks—and sometimes even smells—like food. There are more than five trillion pieces of plastic floating in the ocean, from plastic bags to soda bottles. Some of the plastic is barely visible to the human eye. These microplastics, as they're called, can be the size of a sesame seed or smaller, and while they may not look like much to us, to small fish, like sardines, they look a lot like the plankton the sardines eat. To blue whales, a bit of plastic a few inches long looks like krill, their favorite food. When marine animals spend their energy hunting for food but instead eat plastic that doesn't have any nutritional value, they are left weak and hungry. And eating and digesting plastic can be dangerous for them.

Not only does plastic sometimes deceive sea creatures' eyes, it can also play tricks on their sniffers. Anchovies seek out algae by smell. So, when they encounter algae-covered plastic floating in the sea, the algae and the plastic get gobbled up together in one bite. Similarly, seabirds sometimes mistakenly pick up small bits of plastic covered in plant life, which can harm their health.

# LOOKS ARE DECEIVING.

## PLASTIC IS A DANGEROUS SNACK FOR MARINE LIFE.

SEA TURTLES MISTAKE PLASTIC BAGS FOR JELLYFISH.

# MICROPLASTICS CAUSE MAJOR TROUBLE.

**Q: What are microplastics? And how do they find their way into our water systems?**

**Gregg:** Microplastics are just what they sound like: microscopic pieces of ordinary plastic. Some were made very tiny on purpose, whereas others come from the wearing down of larger pieces. They most often get into our water systems when they're washed down our drains, blown through the air, or dumped as trash into rivers and oceans.

**Q: Is that a problem for fish?**

**Gregg:** You bet it is. Tiny fish and other creatures accidentally eat microplastics, which can fill up their stomachs, making it hard for them to get enough real food. Then bigger animals get a bellyful of all the microplastics and stuck-on toxic chemicals that their little prey have eaten.

**Q: People all over the world eat fish. If we eat fish that are eating plastic, does that mean we're eating plastic?**

**Gregg:** Yup, although it helps us that we take out fishes' guts before eating the fish. [Most of the plastic that fish eat stays in their digestive system.] Some microplastics do make their way into the muscles though, and that's the part we eat most often. It is worth noting that the science is still out on how harmful ingesting plastic really is to humans.

**Q: What are some ways to reduce the amount of microplastics that make their way into the ocean?**

**Gregg:** A lot of our clothes are made of plastic-based fabrics. When we wash them, they break down a bit and microplastics flow from our washing machines into our waterways. So we can help by washing those clothes less often. Another option is to talk to your parents about installing a microplastics filter on your washing machine.

**Q: During your work with Adventure Scientists, what kind of plastic pollution have you observed?**

**Gregg:** Almost 90 percent of the ocean-water samples our volunteers collected from around the world contained microplastics. And more than 90 percent of those microplastics were microfibers from fabrics and fishing nets. But we've also seen large plastic pieces that floated all the way to remote tropical islands.

**GREGG TREINISH,** a National Geographic explorer and founder of Adventure Scientists, which mobilizes people to collect scientific data while they are participating in outdoor activities, is passionate about reducing plastic—especially the teeny-tiny bits called microplastics.

**Q: What are you most hopeful about in the fight against plastic pollution?**

**Gregg:** How easy it is to make progress. Once we're paying attention, there are changes we can make today about the plastics we use and the way we use them. And that's true as a kid, as a school, as a business, or as a country.

MICROPLASTICS LIKE THOSE PICTURED HERE ARE TINY PIECES OF PLASTIC, SOMETIMES SMALLER THAN A SESAME SEED.

## Take Action!

Check the labels on clothes before you buy them and whenever possible, choose ones that use natural fibers, such as cotton, linen, and wool, instead of polyester, which is a type of plastic.

# THE BIG CATCH

During one weekend a year, groups of people around the world gather to clean up beaches and waterways as part of the Ocean Conservancy's International Coastal Cleanup. While they are collecting, they identify every single piece of trash they find and categorize it, which helps pinpoint trends. Here are some of the worst offenders of 2018—all of which were plastic.

MUCH OF THE TRASH PICKED UP BY VOLUNTEERS AT A BEACH CLEANUP WAS PLASTIC.

## FOOD WRAPPERS
### 3,728,712

## STRAWS AND STIRRERS
### 3,668,871

PLASTIC FORKS, KNIVES, OR SPOONS
1,968,065

PLASTIC BEVERAGE BOTTLES
1,754,908

OTHER PLASTIC BAGS
938,929

PLASTIC GROCERY BAGS
964,541

PLASTIC LIDS
728,892

PLASTIC CUPS OR PLATES
656,276

PLASTIC BOTTLE CAPS
1,390,232

**Take Action!**
Join an International Coastal Cleanup event! Ask your parents to check out www.signuptocleanup.org to find volunteer opportunities near you.

# SEA TURTLE
# RESCUE

**A** young green sea turtle bobs along the surface of the water off the coast of Florida. Young turtles usually don't hang out at the surface—that's where predators can easily spot them, plus their food is deeper underwater. But something is keeping this foot (0.3 m)-long turtle from diving.

Luckily, rescuers spot the struggling turtle and take it back to the Clearwater Marine Aquarium, where they name it Chex. Staff place Chex in a shallow kiddie pool so that the turtle won't waste energy trying to dive. They test Chex's blood and run x-rays but can't figure out what's wrong. "Then one day Chex started pooping out something weird," biologist Lauren Bell says. The weird object turns out to be a purple balloon and an attached string.

## SOS (SAVE OUR SEAGRASS!)

Sea turtles often mistake floating trash for food. "Even some *people* can't tell the difference between a plastic grocery bag and a jellyfish in the water," Bell says. But plastic doesn't just hurt sea turtles: It hurts their habitat.

Green sea turtles often hang out close to the shore near seagrass, one of their favorite snacks. Plastic trash left on the beach or coming from rivers that empty into the sea often ends up in this habitat. When it settles on the seagrass, the rubbish can smother the grass, causing it to die. That can mean trouble for green sea turtles like Chex that rely on the seagrass for food or shelter.

## BYE, BALLOON

After several days at the aquarium, Chex starts to improve. Chex eventually passes the entire balloon, plus a two-foot (0.6-m)-long string. A few months later, after aquarium staff have successfully introduced solid food back into Chex's diet, rescuers declare the turtle is ready to return to the sea.

Bell stands hip deep in the waves as another staff member hands Chex to her. She carefully places the little turtle in the water and watches it paddle away. "Chex was like, 'Oh, there's the ocean! OK, bye!'" Bell says. Chex's rescue is worth celebrating ... but maybe without the party balloons.

*RESCUERS SWOOP IN TO HELP A SEA TURTLE THAT SWALLOWED A BALLOON.*

It would take **SIX 10-YEAR-OLDS** to weigh as much as an **AVERAGE-SIZE ADULT GREEN SEA TURTLE.**

# TURTLE POWER

BALLOON STRING

PIECE OF BALLOON

**1** Chex the green sea turtle probably mistook a two-foot (0.6-m)-long balloon string for food.

**2** Chex recovered at the Clearwater Marine Aquarium, spending lots of time in a kiddie pool. Once the turtle started eating solid foods again, rescuers decided Chex was ready to return to the ocean.

A recent study found that **OVER HALF OF ALL SEA TURTLES** have eaten plastic in their lifetime.

**3** Biologist Lauren Bell prepares to release the little turtle back into the sea.

**GREEN SEA TURTLE RESCUE LOCATION**
**Redington Beach, Florida**

NORTH AMERICA
EUROPE
ASIA
PACIFIC OCEAN
ATLANTIC OCEAN
AFRICA
PACIFIC OCEAN
SOUTH AMERICA
INDIAN OCEAN
AUSTRALIA
ANTARCTICA

Seagrass

# DEADLY DEBRIS

There are **250 PIECES OF PLASTIC** in the Great Pacific Garbage Patch for **EVERY HUMAN** on Earth.

## THE INS AND OUTS OF THE (NOT SO) GREAT PACIFIC GARBAGE PATCH

>> On a map, the space between California and Hawai'i looks like an endless blue sea, but in person, you'll find a giant floating island—made up of plastic. Plastic can be found in all the oceans of the world, but currents and winds move marine debris around in certain patterns that create huge concentrations, or "patches," of plastic in some spots. The biggest one—at twice the size of the state of Texas, U.S.A.—is the Great Pacific Garbage Patch. Scientists estimate that there are about 1.8 trillion pieces of plastic in the patch, and 94 percent of them are microplastics. So, don't try walking on it—it's definitely not solid! Some of the patch is made up of bulky items, including fishing gear, like nets, rope, eel traps, crates, and baskets. The patch is also made up of debris washed into the sea during tsunamis. A tsunami, which is a series of waves caused by an earthquake or an undersea volcanic eruption, can pull millions of tons of debris—from cars to household appliances to pieces of houses—off coastlines and into the ocean. Scientists and innovators are working on ways to clean up the patch, although with more plastic constantly entering waterways, the effort will inevitably be ongoing.

TANGLED NYLON ROPE WASHED ASHORE ON THE COAST OF PHUKET, THAILAND.

SMASHED UP SHIPS EVENTUALLY MAKE THEIR WAY TO A SWIRLING MASS OF DEBRIS IN THE GREAT PACIFIC GARBAGE PATCH.

# GARBAGE PATCH ZONES

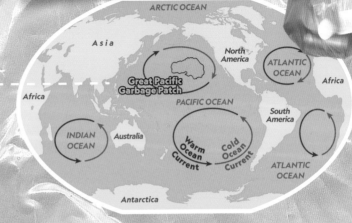

**Garbage patch area with low concentration of plastics**

CANADA
PACIFIC OCEAN
UNITED STATES
California
MEXICO
PACIFIC OCEAN
Hawai'i (United States)

**Garbage patch area with high concentration of plastics**

ARCTIC OCEAN
Asia
North America
ATLANTIC OCEAN
Africa
Great Pacific Garbage Patch
PACIFIC OCEAN
South America
INDIAN OCEAN
Australia
Warm Ocean Current
Cold Ocean Current
ATLANTIC OCEAN
Antarctica

There are five large systems of circulating ocean currents, called gyres, around the world. Plastic and other trash travel with the currents and get trapped in the gyres. The gyre that the Great Pacific Garbage Patch lives in is the largest of them all.

# THE GREAT PACIFIC GARBAGE PATCH MEASURES 618,000 SQUARE MILES.
## (1.6 MILLION SQ KM)

That's about:

**3** TIMES THE SIZE OF FRANCE

**2** TIMES THE SIZE OF TEXAS

# ULTIMATE RECYCLER!

**Eleven-year-old Ryan Hickman's recycling company is saving marine animals.**

RYAN BEGAN COLLECTING RECYCLABLES WHEN HE WAS 3½ YEARS OLD.

At age 11, Ryan Hickman is already a professional recycler. He's been the president of Ryan's Recycling Company since he was 3½ years old. In Southern California, U.S.A., where Ryan lives, recyclables can be traded in for cash at recycling centers. To date, he has collected and recycled 800,000 bottles and cans, which has earned him $85,000. But Ryan isn't in the recycling business for profit. His motivation is helping the planet—including marine animals.

**Q: What kinds of recyclables do you collect?**
**Ryan:** Plastic bottles, aluminum cans, and glass bottles mostly, but I also recycle all sorts of plastic and glass items that don't have a redemption value because it's still important to recycle them.

**Q: Why is it so important to recycle?**
**Ryan:** Recycling keeps items from going into the landfill and the ocean, where they're harmful to the environment and animals. Plus, it saves energy by recycling items instead of creating new ones.

**Q: I bet your friends at school have heard about your recycling company. Has it inspired them to recycle and help you out?**
**Ryan:** I think so. My entire school recycles for me now, and I work to help other schools recycle better, too. Some of the kids also come and help me do beach cleanups.

**Q: What do you do with the money you've earned from recycling?**
**Ryan:** I'm saving it to either buy a full-size recycling truck or for college. I donate all the money from online sales of my shirts to the Pacific Marine Mammal Center [located in Laguna Beach,

Ryan has recycled **115,000 POUNDS (52,200 kg)** of cans and bottles.

RYAN DONATES MONEY FROM THE SALES OF HIS SHIRTS TO A MARINE MAMMAL CENTER IN CALIFORNIA.

California]. So far, I've donated about $10,200 to help them save seals and sea lions that are injured, sick, or starving.

**Q: Why is recycling plastic important for ocean animals?**
**Ryan:** Because if we don't recycle, these items could end up in the ocean. Animals get sick and die from eating the pieces of plastic. It's hard for a sea turtle to know the difference between a jellyfish and a plastic bag. That makes me sad. I want to help do my part to change this.

**Q: Do you have any other tips to help marine animals?**
**Ryan:** I cut up every six-pack ring I find. It's important, because birds, turtles, fish, and other animals get caught in them and then they can't get out.

**Q: What do you wish kids knew more about recycling and plastic?**
**Ryan:** It's super easy to recycle. It might not seem like each of us can do much to save the planet, but when we all do a little bit and work together, we make a huge difference.

# Take Action!

# 4 THINGS YOU CAN DO TO PROTECT MARINE LIFE

**1** **Be proactive!** Cut plastic beverage rings before throwing them away. When you go fishing, be responsible for your fishing supplies. Don't leave fishing line and nets behind, and pick up any that you find.

**2** **Volunteer!** Attend (or help organize) a beach, river, or creek cleanup.

**3** **Pick it up!** When you go to the beach, a river, or a creek, bring a bag to haul away trash and plastic. If everyone who visited the beach picked up 20 pieces of plastic, imagine how much safer our seas would be!

**4** **Seek help:** If you see a marine animal in trouble, don't touch it, try to move it, or feed it. Observe it with a grown-up from at least 50 feet (15 m) away and then describe what you see to a park official, local marine rescue center, or fish and wildlife department.

# TRY! THIS!

## Take a Close Look

On dry land, a jellyfish and a plastic grocery bag may look similar, but you could probably figure out which is which. In the water, though, it gets harder to tell them apart. They're both translucent, and a plastic bag even mimics the way a jellyfish moves through water and follows currents. Microplastics—small plastic pieces that may have broken off larger pieces—can look a bit like krill, a shrimplike crustacean that filter-feeders like blue whales like to eat. They can also look like plankton—tiny, sometimes even microscopic, organisms. See if you can spot the difference between food and plastic through the lens of a marine animal.

## Take Action!

You don't have to live near an ocean to protect animals by picking up plastic waste. The same plastic debris that is a hazard to marine life is a hazard for inland birds and animals—from squirrels and snakes to hawks and bears.

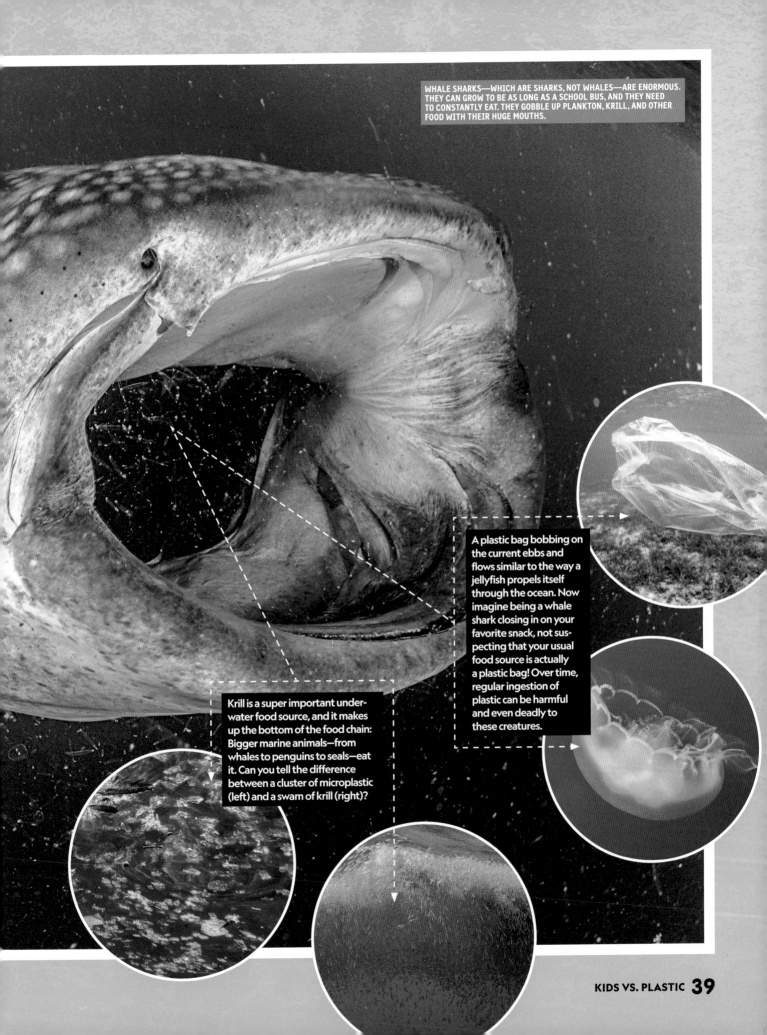

WHALE SHARKS—WHICH ARE SHARKS, NOT WHALES—ARE ENORMOUS. THEY CAN GROW TO BE AS LONG AS A SCHOOL BUS, AND THEY NEED TO CONSTANTLY EAT. THEY GOBBLE UP PLANKTON, KRILL, AND OTHER FOOD WITH THEIR HUGE MOUTHS.

A plastic bag bobbing on the current ebbs and flows similar to the way a jellyfish propels itself through the ocean. Now imagine being a whale shark closing in on your favorite snack, not suspecting that your usual food source is actually a plastic bag! Over time, regular ingestion of plastic can be harmful and even deadly to these creatures.

Krill is a super important underwater food source, and it makes up the bottom of the food chain: Bigger marine animals—from whales to penguins to seals—eat it. Can you tell the difference between a cluster of microplastic (left) and a swam of krill (right)?

PICKING UP TRASH KEEPS PLASTIC
FROM ENTERING WATERWAYS.

# CHAPTER 3

# WASTE WARRIORS

>> **TACKLING PLASTIC POLLUTION IS GOING TO TAKE A GLOBAL—AND CREATIVE—EFFORT.** People of all ages all over the world are finding unique and inspiring ways to reduce, reuse, recycle, and clean up plastic. They are also using their voices to speak up against plastic waste. Read on to learn inspiring stories about citizens doing their part to combat plastic, and to find out what you can do to be part of the movement.

# ALL IN IT
# TOGETHER

Cities and countries around the world are taking a stand to ban single-use plastic (think thin plastic grocery bags, plastic lids on fountain sodas, and straws). Here is a sampling of these efforts:

**Seattle:** In 2018, the city banned plastic straws and plastic utensils at restaurants.

**San Francisco:** First city in the U.S. to ban plastic bags. Since the 2007 ban, there has been a 72 percent reduction in plastic bag pollution.

**San Diego:** In 2018, the city banned the use of plastic-foam food and drink containers.

**Washington, D.C.:** In 2010, it became the first major city to enact a bag fee, charging 5 cents for paper and plastic bags. Revenue from the tax goes to clean up the Anacostia River.

**Vancouver:** In 2018, the city banned plastic straws and plastic-foam cups and take-out containers.

**United Kingdom:** In 2018, the U.K. decided to ban all plastic straws and plastic cotton swab handles beginning in 2020.

**Bangladesh:** Banned single-use plastic bags in 2002, the first country to do so.

**Hamburg:** Banned single-use coffee pods in 2016.

**Karnataka:** Banned plastic bags and plastic utensils in 2018.

**Vanuatu:** The island nation announced in 2017 that it was phasing out single-use plastic bags and plastic bottles.

**Peru:** In 2019, visitors were banned from bringing single-use plastic into the country's natural and cultural protected areas, like Machu Picchu.

**Zimbabwe:** Banned plastic-foam take-out containers in 2017, charging violators a fine of $30 to $500.

**Kenya:** As of 2017, those who violate the plastic bag ban face a fine of up to $38,000 or four years in jail.

**Chile:** Banned single-use plastic bags in 2018, the first country in South America to do so.

### Map labels

ARCTIC OCEAN

**Vancouver** Canada
**Seattle** Washington United States
**San Francisco** California United States
**San Diego** California United States
NORTH AMERICA
**Washington, D.C.** United States
ATLANTIC OCEAN
PACIFIC OCEAN
**PERU**
SOUTH AMERICA
**CHILE**

**UNITED KINGDOM**
EUROPE
**Hamburg** Germany
ASIA
AFRICA
**Karnataka** India
**BANGLADESH**
PACIFIC OCEAN
**KENYA**
INDIAN OCEAN
**ZIMBABWE**
**VANUATU**
AUSTRALIA

ANTARCTICA

# THIS TO THAT

One New York City restaurant lets customers borrow reusable take-out containers.

Just because your order is to go, that doesn't mean the packaging has to go straight into the trash. There are some pretty simple alternatives to single-use plastic.

## ALTERNATIVES TO PLASTIC AND PLASTIC-FOAM TO-GO CONTAINERS

**Compostable plates**

**Plastic plates**

### TIP!
Skip the plastic plates the next time you throw a party and look for paper plates that can be composted with food waste and yard clippings.

**Reusable plastic or glassware you bring from home**

**Plastic and Plastic-foam to-go containers**

## Metal straw and lid

### TIP!

When you place your order, request your beverage without a straw or lid. It's a simple way to save a lot of plastic. Even better: Bring a cup from home and ask if your drink can be put in it instead.

## Plastic straw and lid

### TIP!

Keep a reusable bag in your backpack and in the trunk of your family's car, so you're never caught empty-handed at the checkout.

## Reusable bag

## Plastic bag

## Metal utensils

### TIP!

There's nothing better than bringing leftovers home from your favorite restaurant, but that feeling isn't quite as sweet when you're handed a plastic-foam to-go container. Bring your own reusable container from home to load up with leftovers.

### TIP!

Decline the plastic utensils that restaurants automatically put in the to-go bag and use your own metal utensils when you get home.

## Plastic utensils

# CREATIVE CLEANUPS

**R**aising awareness and getting people inspired to clean up and recycle plastic require thinking outside the box. Here are three next-level inventions that are paying it forward and turning heads.

## ALL EYES ON TRASH

High-heeled shoes, footballs, plastic water bottles—Mr. Trash Wheel "eats" them all. This googly-eyed machine sits at the end of the 18-mile (29-km)-long Jones Falls stream in Baltimore, Maryland, U.S.A. Solar panels and the water's current turn the barge's wheel, which then scoops up litter and places it into a dumpster. When the dumpster is full, a boat tows it away, and it's replaced by a new dumpster. Later, the trash is burned at a nearby waste-to-energy plant to power nearby homes.

## PEDALING FOR PLASTIC

Like many of the world's waterways, London's River Thames is littered with plastic. To raise awareness—and help clean up the river—Dhruv Boruah invented a contraption that allows him to "cycle" on the river while picking up trash with his grabber tool. Here's how it works: A bicycle (Dhruv handmade his from bamboo!) is attached to two inflated pontoons and equipped with a rudder and a pedal-powered propeller, which allows Dhruv to pedal on the river. He grabs trash as he pedals and deposits it into baskets attached to his bike. He says his invention is a great conversation starter for the people he meets on his rides, prompting discussions about the importance of keeping the river plastic free.

## MAKING A SPLASH FOR PLASTIC

While Dhruv Boruah raises awareness about plastic from atop the River Thames, Lindsey Cole is working toward the same goal from in the water. Cole swam 120 miles (193 km) of the Thames—wearing two wet suits and a mermaid tail! Swimming about four hours a day for 21 days, Cole was followed by an artist friend in a support canoe, which towed a hollow sculpture of a mermaid made of plastic bottles. Cole asked passersby to pick up litter and put it in the sculpture, as a visual representation of how much plastic is in the water, and to help save animals from eating or getting caught in it.

DHRUV BORUAH PEDALS WHILE HE PICKS UP PLASTIC FROM THE RIVER THAMES.

LINDSEY COLE POSES IN HER MERMAID TAIL WITH HER PLASTIC SCULPTURE.

# Take Action!

## FIND AN ANSWER IN ART

Is there a plastic problem in your community? Maybe there are a lot of plastic bags and bottles in your neighborhood creek. Or maybe the school's recycling bins are being ignored. Put on your creativity cap to think up new ways to raise awareness to help find a solution!

**1** **Gather a group of friends** to make a sculpture out of recyclables and show it off at a community event or enter it in a local arts contest.

**2** **Write a piece of poetry** about a plastic issue that's bothering you and read it at a local poetry slam or open mic event.

**3** **Ask your teacher** or principal if you can decorate the school recycling bins to make them more eye-catching and recycling friendly.

MR. TRASH WHEEL "EATS" PLASTIC FROM A STREAM IN BALTIMORE, MARYLAND.

# PLANET PROTECTOR

# ULTIMATE RECYCLER!

## This teen is all "fore" plastic cleanup.

In 2017, then 16-year-old Alex Weber was exploring a cove with her dad off California's Pebble Beach. Alex is a free diver, which means she holds her breath and swims underwater with just a mask and fins, and does not use a scuba tank. During one dive, she discovered something quite unexpected—thousands of golf balls lining the ocean floor. This stretch of Central California coastline is home to a handful of golf courses, and inevitably, some balls are hit or roll into the ocean. Alex began collecting the balls in mesh bags and hauling them to shore using a kayak. Once she had filled her garage with huge bins of them, she decided to do something about the problem.

**Q: What did you think when you saw how many golf balls were on the ocean floor?**
**Alex:** It was absolutely shocking. I had no idea the golf balls were there to begin with. We were in the Monterey Bay National Marine Sanctuary, and to see a huge patch of the seafloor covered with white golf balls that were rolling around was unbelievable.

**Q: Was your immediate instinct to haul the golf balls to shore?**
**Alex:** Yes. I had been doing a lot of beach cleanups. This brought my passion of picking up trash and being under the ocean together.

**Q: How do you clean up the golf balls?**
**Alex:** You have to pick them up one at a time. Golf balls are barely buoyant, so it's like trying to catch a feather on a windy day. I gather them in a mesh bag, come up for a breath of air, and then dive back down. I put all the bags in a kayak until it can barely still float, and then I tow it back to shore.

**Q: How many golf balls have you collected so far?**
**Alex:** 50,000.

**Q: Wow! But you didn't just collect them—you started studying the effect of them on the ocean. How did that come about?**
**Alex:** I noticed that the golf balls that I collected and stored in my garage smelled. I reached out to a scientist from Stanford University—Matt Savoca—to find out why. He explained that when you put plastic in the ocean, it's like putting a sponge in the

ALEX AND HER FRIENDS BRAINSTORM AN ART INSTALLATION PIECE THAT USES THE COLLECTED GOLF BALLS TO RAISE AWARENESS ABOUT OCEAN POLLUTION.

ALEX FREE DIVES—HOLDING HER BREATH AND SWIMMING UNDERWATER WITH JUST A MASK AND FINS—TO GATHER GOLF BALLS.

ocean. The golf balls absorb chemicals in the water and start to smell like food that animals like to eat. The animals are drawn to the plastic and eat it. Matt said I should write a paper about it, and I said, "I'm 16! I have no idea how to do that!" He took me under his wing and taught me how.

**Q: And you published your findings in a scientific journal! What did you find out?**
**Alex:** That over time, golf balls wear down and break into microplastics. We were also able to pinpoint "hot spots," where the golf balls are. It was the first study on golf balls' effect on the ocean, and it brought awareness to an issue that people hadn't heard about.

**Q: What have you learned from cleaning up 50,000 golf balls?**
**Alex:** If you see something that doesn't seem right, question it more. Don't shut down the curiosity in your mind. Ask why things are the way they are. Don't be afraid to identify a problem in your community. If everyone does something little, our world will be a more beautiful place.

MARINE ANIMALS OFTEN MISTAKE PLASTIC—INCLUDING PLASTIC-COATED GOLF BALLS—FOR FOOD.

# CHIPPING AWAY AT THE PLASTIC PROBLEM

## STUDENTS IN INDIA DEMAND A CHANGE IN POTATO CHIP PACKAGING.

Sometimes a great place to start combating plastic pollution is close to home. Like, say, your school cafeteria.

To demonstrate just how much single-use plastic is routinely discarded, a group of students at an all-girls school in the city of Madurai in southern India collected all the food wrappers they used in a two-week period, which tallied up to more than 20,000. They then sent them back to the manufacturers that made the products—which ranged from potato chips to candy to crackers—and included a note that said that while they were happy with the taste and quality of the products, they were less happy with the packaging. Seeing just how much plastic was being tossed after the snacks inside were eaten was a powerful reminder to the companies that the packaging they use has a major impact on the environment. The students requested that a more eco-friendly packaging be used in the future. One of the companies responded to the students' letter, saying that while it understood the effects of the packaging, it had not yet found a solution to the issue. The project was a way for the kids to bring attention to the problem of single-use plastic problem and hold the companies that make such packaging more accountable for what they produce.

It takes a **CONVENTIONAL POTATO CHIP** wrapper about 80 years to break down.

ENVIRONMENTAL ACTIVISM ON A LARGE SCALE—LIKE THE STUDENTS SENDING 20,000 WRAPPERS TO MANUFACTURERS—CAN HAVE THE A GREAT EFFECT. ACTIVISM DONE ON A LARGE SCALE CAN TURN HEADS AND MOTIVATE PEOPLE OR COMPANIES TO MAKE A CHANGE.

# ENGLISH COMPANY GOES OUT ON A LIMB FOR ALTERNATIVE POTATO CHIP PACKAGING.

**Money doesn't grow on trees,** but now some potato chip wrappers do. The problem with most potato chip packaging is that it's made of a mix of materials (plastic and aluminum foil) that can't be separated out and recycled. Scientists have struggled to find a replacement that keeps food clean and fresh—and is still lightweight. Now a small potato chip company from England called Two Farmers has found an unexpected alternative— eucalyptus trees.

MARK GREEN (LEFT) AND SEAN MASON, FOUNDERS OF TWO FARMERS

The company created biodegradable potato chip bags using eucalyptus wood pulp that decomposes in just 26 weeks!

**1**

**2**

# KIDS HAVE A SAY.

**S**peak up! Kids are a crucial part of the movement to reduce plastic pollution. Your voice is important and, thankfully, there are lots of people listening. Here are some ideas to help you speak out about reducing plastic.

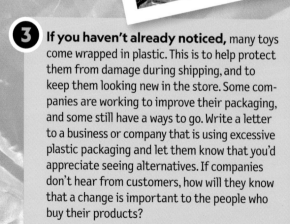

**1** **If you notice** that one of your family's favorite restaurants only offers plastic utensils, ask your parents to help you talk to the manager or owner about replacing plastic with metal or compostable utensils. You can also put your words on paper. Write a letter and send it to the owner or CEO.

**2** **If you go to a restaurant** that is doing a good job avoiding distribution of single-use plastic, let the staff know you've noticed! Tell the waitstaff, cashier, and manager that you appreciate it. This encourages them to keep up the good work.

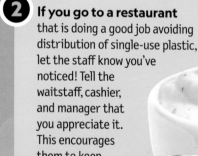

**3** **If you haven't already noticed,** many toys come wrapped in plastic. This is to help protect them from damage during shipping, and to keep them looking new in the store. Some companies are working to improve their packaging, and some still have a ways to go. Write a letter to a business or company that is using excessive plastic packaging and let them know that you'd appreciate seeing alternatives. If companies don't hear from customers, how will they know that a change is important to the people who buy their products?

Dear [Name of the owner of the business],

My name is [Fill in your name here], and I am writing because I wanted to let you know how I feel about the use of plastic in your [Fill in: store/restaurant/business, etc.].

When I recently visited your business, I noticed that only [Fill in: plastic utensils, plastic to-go containers, plastic bags, etc.] were offered. Single-use plastic is often non-recyclable and can end up in our oceans. As a customer, I encourage you to offer sustainable options, like [Fill in: metal flatware, biodegradable to-go containers, etc.]. Thank you for your consideration.

Sincerely,

[Sign your name here.]

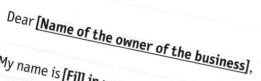

# THESE ALTERNATIVE PLASTIC UTENSILS ARE THE PITS.

Most plastic utensils aren't recyclable, but a company in Mexico has invented a way to make some that decompose in just 240 days. How did the company do it? It turned to an unlikely material—avocado pits. Avocado pits are typically discarded after the flesh is scooped out, but the Mexican company studied the pits and discovered they contain a molecular compound that can be molded like synthetic plastic. The company processes the pits and turns them into utensils. Turning avocados into utensils is a great way to—quite literally—go green!

# TRY! THIS!

Take this personality quiz to find out which marine animal you're most like—and then read a tip on how you can protect that animal from plastic.

## PERSONALITY QUIZ

Remember, if these descriptions don't match your personality, don't worry. The questions are just for fun!

**START HERE!**

Are you more likely to **GO WITH THE CROWD**, or do you prefer to **FLY SOLO?**

CROWD, FOR SURE

FLY SOLO!

Choose your next vacation destination.

SUPER-SPOOKY GHOST TOWN

SUNNY TROPICAL ISLAND

Would you rather have a long neck like a giraffe or be able to turn your head around like an owl?

GIRAFFE

OWL

Pick a single-use plastic item to ditch from your daily life.

Where would you rather spend your evening?

JUST THE STARS ABOVE ME

BRIGHT LIGHTS, BIG CITY!

CHEETAH

OCTOPUS

CHOOSE ONE: Cook a big breakfast and be late for school, or grab something quick but make it on time.

Which would you rather snack on?

CHOCOLATE BAR

GUMMY BEARS

Would you rather run as fast as a cheetah or hide as well as an octopus?

You're helping NASA with its Mars mission. What's your job?

DESIGNING THE SPACECRAFT

I'D BE AN ASTRONAUT, OBVIOUSLY.

Pick a single-use plastic item to ditch from your daily life.

**PLASTIC BOTTLES**

**PLASTIC CARRY-OUT CONTAINERS**

**PLASTIC SIX-PACK RINGS**

**EAT, OF COURSE!**

**BE ON TIME, DUH.**

**PLASTIC BALLOONS**

**PLASTIC BAGS**

### BOTTLENOSE DOLPHIN

Just like the bottlenose dolphin, you're known for being playful. You enjoy meeting new people and spending time in a pod, er, group. Dolphins talk to each other a lot—just like you and your friends. (Well, kind of ... dolphins communicate with whistles, clicks, and squawks.)
**HELP PROTECT DOLPHINS:** Cut up six-pack soda rings so dolphins and other marine animals can't get tangled in them.

### WHITE-FACED WHISTLING DUCK

You know how to crank up the volume. Similarly, this duck's high-pitched whistling calls are hard to miss. And you're not afraid of change: New school? No prob. These ducks are also OK with exploring new places. Though typically found in the water, they're called "tree ducks" because they can sometimes be found perched in branches.
**HELP PROTECT DUCKS:** Ducks can consume microbeads found in certain cleaners and toothpastes. Check the products you use for ingredients that have "poly" in their name to see if they are made with these tiny plastics.

### HARBOR SEAL

This marine mammal is big on routine, and so are you. Harbor seals spend a lot of time switching between napping in groups and hunting on the beach. Sticking to a schedule doesn't mean you're not full of surprises, though. Like harbor seals, you occasionally let your curiosity lead the way.
**HELP PROTECT SEALS:** Seals get caught in fishing nets and line. When you go fishing, make sure you don't leave any gear in the water or near the shore.

### WHALE SHARK

Like the whale shark, you can be quiet and mysterious. But you're just saving your words for when they count. When you do speak up, people listen— you've got some serious leadership potential. Whale sharks are pretty impressive, too; this boneless giant is the world's largest fish.
**HELP PROTECT SHARKS:** Whale sharks mistake plastic bags for food. Skip the plastic bag at the store and bring your own reusable one instead.

### GREEN SEA TURTLE

Green sea turtles are often on the go—just like you. They migrate long distances between their feeding grounds and their nesting sites, up to 1,600 miles (2,575 km). That's farther than New York City is from Dallas, Texas! Although you love to travel, home is a special spot. These turtles might feel the same way. When it's time to lay their eggs, females return to the same nesting grounds where they were born.
**HELP PROTECT TURTLES:** Sea turtles mistake balloons— which can drop from the air and land in the sea—as food. Don't release helium balloons, and consider an alternative decoration to balloons at parties—like flowers or paper lanterns.

FROM GLASS FOOD CONTAINERS TO BAMBOO BOWLS, A VARIETY OF ALTERNATIVES CAN HELP YOU CUT DOWN ON THE AMOUNT OF PLASTIC IN YOUR DAILY LIFE!

# CHAPTER 4

# PARING DOWN ON PLASTIC

>> **WITH EFFORT, WE CAN REPLACE A LOT OF THE PLASTIC WE USE IN OUR EVERYDAY LIFE** with nonplastic alternatives. Is it possible to live entirely plastic free? Most people agree that it's next to impossible to completely cut plastic from our lives—partly because there are some upsides to it. Read about one family's efforts to limit single-use plastic from even entering their home, then learn more about the types of plastic products that literally save lives, and the types you may be able to do without.

# THIS TO THAT

## SINGLE-USE PLASTIC ALTERNATIVES

>>>

The average student throws away 67 pounds (31 kg) of lunch packaging waste every year.

A lot of the plastic we use is simply out of convenience. With a little bit of planning, though, most plastic items can be swapped for something that's better for the environment. Check out how to switch from these everyday single-use plastic products to more planet-friendly ones.

**Mesh reusable bag**

>>>

**Plastic produce bag**

**TIP!**
Bring broccoli or a bunch of apples home in a reusable mesh bag instead of a single-use plastic one.

**TIP!**
Instead of packing your trail mix in a throwaway plastic bag, use a reusable metal container.

**Plastic sandwich bag**

**Beeswax wrap**

**TIP!**
Cover a bowl or a half-used lemon with reusable beeswax wrap—made from a blend of cotton and beeswax—instead of plastic cling wrap.

**Plastic cling wrap**

**Mason Jar**

**TIP!**
Put a piece of paper over the rim of a mason jar, then screw on the metal ring. Poke a reusable straw through the paper and—voilà!—you have a cute drinking cup!

**Disposable plastic cup**

**Metal container**

**TIP!**
Save a plastic cup and plastic spoon and eat your ice cream in a cone container!

**Ice-cream cone**

**Ice cream in a cup**

# WHAT ABOUT MY TOYS?

## HOW TO PLAY WITH LESS PLASTIC

**R**eady to go plastic free? There's one major hurdle that may be hard to get over: toys! From action figures to balls to board game pieces, it's hard to find a toy that's not made, at least in part, with plastic. That's because plastic toys are durable and easy to clean. But there are some ways to play with less plastic. Check out these options.

### BUY TOYS MADE FROM NATURAL MATERIALS.
Seek out playthings made of alternatives to plastic, such as a cotton jump rope or a wooden dollhouse.

### EMBRACE HAND-ME-DOWNS.
Reusing plastic is better than buying new plastic. Ask your parents if you can hit up garage sales or secondhand stores instead of getting new toys at the store. Or organize a toy swap with friends.

### PAY ATTENTION TO PACKAGING.
When you do buy new toys—for yourself or, say, for a birthday party—look for ones that aren't packaged in loads of plastic.

SHOP FOR TOYS THAT USE MINIMAL PLASTIC PACKAGING.

BACK TO BASICS: TOYS MADE FROM NATURAL MATERIALS ARE ONE ALTERNATIVE TO PLASTIC.

**GOOD NEWS!** Some popular toy-makers like Hasbro, the **MAKER OF NERF,** are beginning to **PHASE OUT** plastic packaging.

About **90 PERCENT** of all toys are made with plastic.

# "GREENER" PLASTIC TOYS

**Reducing plastic is all fun and games** until you realize some of your favorite toys are made of plastic—including Lego pieces. But there's good news on the horizon: By 2030, Lego plans to make most of its pieces out of a plant-based material sourced from sugarcane husks that looks and acts like plastic but decomposes faster. So far, the company has released a line of the eco-friendly pieces that (appropriately) look like plants, with more to come.

WHILE THIS LEGO TREE IS STILL PLASTIC, PLANT-BASED PIECES ARE ON THEIR WAY!

**Another company, Green Toys,** makes its plastic toys—from trucks to bath toys to tea sets—from recycled milk jugs! To date, the company has repurposed more than 80 million milk jugs, which are washed and shredded into flakes and processed into a raw material to turn it into a toy. And all the toys' packaging is made from recyclable cardboard or recycled water bottles.

REHOME YOUR OLD TOYS BY DONATING OR RESELLING THEM.

SPRING sale

## Take Action!

Don't toss that toy! There are many organizations that accept used toys and resell them or give them away. Some websites tailored to individual towns and neighborhoods let you post items for free that you're offering up. Just make sure to ask a grown-up for help.

Jump Rope

green toys

THE HANDLES ARE ACTUALLY RECYCLED MILK JUGS!

Most of the time, reducing your plastic consumption is a good thing, but not all plastic is bad. It can be lifesaving and—believe it or not—there are some types of plastic that even have a hand in helping the environment. Check out the plastic products that made it onto the "good for us" list.

# THE BEST OF PLASTIC

**MEDICAL TUBES:** Plastic medical tubes deliver oxygen, blood, and medicine to patients.

**GLASSES:** Plastic can help you see! If you wear glasses, the lenses—and possibly even your frames—are made of plastic. Contact lenses are made from plastic as well.

**BIKE HELMET:** Your bike helmet is mostly made of plastic. It's lightweight, but it is still really good at absorbing shock and protecting your brain if you fall off your bike and hit your head.

**Your old glasses** can give someone else a new look! When you pick out your next set of frames, ask your eyeglass shop if it works with an organization that collects used ones. You can also find several groups online that freshen up frames, add new lenses, and then give them to someone in need.

**EPIPEN:** An epinephrine auto-injector, known by the brand name EpiPen, is a medical device used to inject medicine into a person having a serious allergic reaction to things like bee stings, bug bites, or food. EpiPens, which are partly made of plastic, keep the medicine inside sterile, meaning free of germs.

**CARS:** Cars aren't made completely of plastic—they have strong carbon steel or aluminum alloy frames. However, about 50 percent of a new car's total volume is plastic, including panels and bumpers. Plastic bounces back better than metal and is less likely to dent. It also doesn't rust. Perhaps more important, it is lightweight. As cars were designed using more plastic, they became lighter, improving gas mileage, which saves fossil fuels.

**AIRBAGS:** In some car accidents, cushions called airbags pop out of the car's steering wheel and dashboard to protect passengers' heads. These cushions, which instantly inflate, are made of nylon, a type of plastic.

# STUDENT HAS VISION FOR COFFEE GROUNDS.

**While working in a coffee shop** in Scotland, Ryan Davren saw firsthand all the waste that comes with making coffee. After coffee is brewed, the ground-up beans are usually dumped. Then Ryan thought of a better use for them: eyeglasses. He tried mixing the coffee grounds with flax seed. After this mixture dries, it has a texture similar to that of wood. Ryan was able to cast the material and turned it into biodegradable eyeglass frames.

GLASSES FRAMES MADE FROM COFFEE WASTE BY UNIVERSITY OF DUNDEE STUDENT RYAN DAVREN

# PLANET PROTECTOR

# LIVING (NEARLY) PLASTIC FREE: FOR REAL!

**This family is the extreme team when it comes to reducing waste.**

For the Leblond family, reducing plastic from their day-to-day life isn't just a priority; it's a lifestyle. Katelin and Kevin Leblond and their kids, Phoenix, 7, and Cleo, 5, don't have trash pickup at their house. Ever. In fact, the Canadian family is so good at refusing to use throwaway items—and recycling and composting the rest—that they can fit all the trash they accumulate in one year in one or two large jars! Find out how these amazing plastic warriors do it.

**Q: How long have you been striving to cut down on waste?**
**Katelin:** Since 2014. Before that, we were putting a large black garbage bag out for curbside pickup weekly. Over time, and with gradual changes, we no longer needed pickup, and we cut our recycling by at least 50 percent. We also compost.

**COMPOST BECOMES SOIL, WHICH CAN BE USED IN A GARDEN.**

**Q: What were some of the first steps you took to reduce plastic from your life?**
**Katelin:** I started by no longer purchasing produce wrapped in plastic, berries in plastic containers, and prewashed salad in plastic bags. I started to frequent the bulk section of the grocery store for grains, nuts, dried fruit, and even chocolate. I started to shop differently—instead of a one-stop shop at a chain grocer, I found a bakery that allows me to use a pillowcase for bread and a butcher who allowed me to use my own containers, and I started to shop at local shops and farmers markets.

**Q: Was there an area in your life that you realized you were using the most plastic?**
**Katelin:** Definitely the kitchen and bathroom. While grocery stores are starting to change packaging, most still sell food and personal care items heavily packaged in plastic. I realized that, in our bathroom closet, there were different shampoos for me, my husband, the kids—we even had specific shampoo for our dog. We stopped purchasing 99 percent of the items we used to use in the bathroom.

CLOTH BAGS CAN BE USED INSTEAD OF SINGLE-USE PLASTIC ONES.

**Watch out for this new trend: Plastic-free aisles in grocery stores!**

Items are sold in bulk and customers bring their own jars, containers, and reusable bags to load up on everything from food to shampoo to laundry detergent. Packaged items are made from recyclable paper, cardboard, glass, or metal.

**Q: What do you use instead?**
**Katelin:** I make homemade toothpaste, body cream, and sunscreen. We use a shampoo and conditioner bar for our hair and bar soap for our bodies and hands.

**Q: What are the biggest challenges about going nearly plastic free?**
**Katelin:** You need to be willing to change your habits, shop differently, and keep an open, positive mind to the options that you still do have. For kids, the greatest challenge might be changing habits and expectations where toys and snack foods are concerned.

**Q: You added two "Rs" to reduce, reuse, and recycle. What are they?**
**Katelin:** Refuse and rot. Refuse comes before reduce, reuse, and recycle. It basically keeps your goal of zero waste in check. Refuse to purchase or accept anything you do not need—like plastic grocery bags and coffee cups, "free" items like pens and stickers, and free tasters that come in single-use plastic serving vessels.

Rot simply refers to composting. This is such a massive step in reducing the amount of waste a household sends to the landfill. Compost becomes soil and nutrients for gardens and farms.

**Q: Your family fits your year's supply of trash in one or two big jars. What's in there?**
**Katelin:** Receipts, stickers, plastic tags from clothing, foil wrappers from road trip snacks, bandages, dental floss, bristles from toothbrushes, ribbon, and twine. We are learning to embrace minimalism, although this is work in progress!

## TAKE THE JAR CHALLENGE!

**It takes the Leblond family a year** to fill one to two large jars with all their household trash. How long will it take your family to fill a jar?

Haul one out from your family's recycling, rinse it, and put it on the kitchen counter. Instead of throwing something in the trash, toss it into the jar. Can your family keep from filling it up in an hour? A day? A week? Once your jar is full, empty it and try again.

See if you and your family can find ways to produce less trash and beat your record!

# PASS ON PLASTIC.

## HOW TO PLAN A PLASTIC-FREE PARTY

Plates, cups, utensils, wrapping paper, balloons, gift bags ... plastic can feel like an uninvited party crasher! Believe it or not, you can throw a party without a bunch of plastic. Here are some tips to keep the trash bins from filling up at your next bash.

### USE THE REAL THING.
Instead of disposable cups, plates, and utensils, use real ones. Need more serving supplies? Hit up a thrift store for retro plates and cups.

### SKIP THE GOODIE BAGS.
Take a hard pass on goodie bags. Not only are goodie bags usually plastic, they are often filled with even more plastic, like trinkets. Instead, you could send guests home with one of those cool cups you found at the thrift store and a home-baked treat, or make individual paper fortune-tellers for each of your friends.

### BUY IN BULK.
Ask your parents to buy party food in bulk. Individually wrapped foods, including snack-size bags of chips, use more packaging. You know what also uses less packaging? Things made at home. Slice up fruit and veggies and put them on a serving platter. Pop some popcorn and pour it into a big bowl. Make a big pitcher of lemonade and put it out with a stack of washable cups.

CHOPPED FRESH FRUIT AND HOMEMADE BAKED GOODS ELIMINATE PLASTIC WASTE.

# HOW TO MAKE A "THANK YOU" FORTUNE-TELLER

Send your party guests home with a little bit of fun! These fortune-tellers are easy to make and can be personalized to match your party's theme. All you need is plain paper, some crayons or colored pencils, and scissors.

**1** Fold the bottom of the paper to the side of the page to make a triangle.

**2** Use scissors to cut off the flap at the top.

cut off

**3** Open the triangle and you will have a square.

**4** Fold one corner of the paper diagonally to the other corner.

**5** Open your paper. You will now have a center point marked on the paper.

**6** Fold each corner of the paper toward the center.

**7** When all four corners have been folded, your fortune-teller should look like this.

**8** Turn the paper over so that the folded sides are face down. Then fold all the corners to the center diagonally.

**9** Once you have folded in the four corners, write the numbers one through eight on each of the triangles.

**10** Turn the folded paper over and make each outside square a different color.

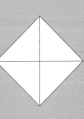

**11** The main center square can say, "Thank you for coming to my party!" The fortunes can say: You rock!; BFF; Team Awesome; My Hero; Dream Big; Gold Star; Good Vibes; and Bestie.

## I Spy Plastic in the Bathroom.

**Uh-oh, this bathroom has a single-use-plastic problem. See if you can find the trouble spots!**

You can run, but you can't hide from plastic. Especially in the bathroom. Look for 15 items hanging out in this bathroom made at least in part of plastic. Check the answer key to see how you did.

THIS SHARK IS MADE FROM BITS OF DISCARDED PLASTIC.

# CHAPTER 5

# PLASTIC REPACKAGED

**THE NEXT BEST THING TO ELIMINATING PLASTIC IS EXTENDING** the life of the plastic you already have. About 40 percent of new plastic is designed to be disposable—to be used just once, then tossed. Why not find something to do with this plastic? It could be as easy as rinsing out a plastic to-go container and using it again for leftovers. Or consider giving upcycling a try: That's when you take something that would normally be tossed or recycled and turn it into something new. If you use your imagination, the contents of your recycling bin could be the start of a rainy-day fantastical sculpture project. Find out more ways to extend the life of plastic.

# THREADS
# FROM THE SEA

**OCEAN TRASH IS BEING UPCYCLED INTO SHOES AND CLOTHING.**

**W**hy send plastic to the landfill when you can wear it instead? That's the idea that's inspiring some fashion companies to create clothing lines and shoes made from recycled plastic. Plastic bottles and other types of plastic can be turned into a material that looks and acts like thread. Here's how it works: It all starts with a bunch of plastic water bottles that are crushed up into tiny pieces and then washed. Then these pieces are turned into filament that can be mixed with cotton, canvas, or rubber. The process has been used to make shoes, shirts, jackets, and other clothing. Transforming plastic into something you wear not only extends the life of the plastic, it also turns your wardrobe into an awesome advertisement for the importance of reducing plastic waste.

WORKERS FROM THE NATIONAL OCEANIC AND ATMOSPHERIC ADMINISTRATION (NOAA) HAUL AWAY FISHING NETS THAT WASHED ASHORE ON MIDWAY ATOLL IN THE PACIFIC OCEAN.

# QUIZ!

Do you have an eye for upcycled fashion? Guess which pieces of clothing were once a plastic bottle, and then check your answers below.

**①** **②** **③** **④** **⑤** **⑥** **⑦** **⑧** **⑨** **⑩**

**Answers**
**Once a plastic bottle:** 1. sunglasses; 2. sandals; 3. blue runway dresses; 4. fleece jackets; 8. message T-shirt; 9. running shoes  **Non-recycled clothing:** 5. men's shirts; 6. denim jeans; 7. down jacket; 10. knit scarf

**KIDS VS. PLASTIC 73**

# THIS TO THAT

28 percent of parents admit to throwing away toys that are in working order, a U.K. survey found.

Does your bedroom need a makeover? Instead of shopping for new knickknacks and store-bought baubles, look at what you already have and repurpose these items into something creative and fresh!

...into a mini succulent planter

**Rubber ducky**

**TIP!**
Infuse some life into your rubber ducky! Cut a hole in the ducky's back and fill it with soil. Plant a tiny succulent and watch it grow!

...into a jewelry holder

**Plastic stegosaur**

**TIP!**
Put those spiky stegosaur plates to work. Paint a dinosaur toy with sparkly paint or a color to match your room's aesthetic, and then drape bracelets, necklaces, or rings from it.

...into
key holder

**Lego toys**

≫≫

**TIP!**

Use your expert Lego-building skills to create this key holder. Design the base to suit your style and top it with your favorite Lego figurine. Then use a Lego "coupling plate" to attach to a key ring. Snap your keys onto the base for safekeeping!

...into
drawer knobs

**Plastic
animals figures**

≫≫

**TIP!**

Give your dresser a fresh look by swapping out the knobs with some plastic toys, like safari animal figurines.

# A BRIGHT IDEA

## IN THE PHILIPPINES, PLASTIC BOTTLES ARE UPCYCLED AS "LIGHTBULBS."

**P**lastic bottles can mean the difference between darkness and light in some homes in the Philippines. In parts of the country, where electricity isn't available or is too expensive to use, volunteers are installing discarded plastic bottles on rooftops, which are then turned into lightbulbs. Here's how it works: Clear plastic bottles are filled with water and then attached to a small metal brace. Volunteers and government workers cut a hole in the roof of a house, and the bottle and brace are inserted. Then sealant is used around the brace to keep the roof from leaking. With the help of the bright sun, the makeshift bulbs give off about 55 watts of light—the same as a standard lightbulb. The brilliant part? No electricity is used. Light passes through the bottle and refracts off the water inside, spreading light into the room below. The bottles are considered safer than using candles, which can be a fire hazard, and the plastic bottles used are ones that otherwise would have been sent to the landfill.

A VOLUNTEER INSTALLS A PLASTIC BOTTLE "LIGHT" THAT WILL ILLUMINATE THIS MAN'S HOME.

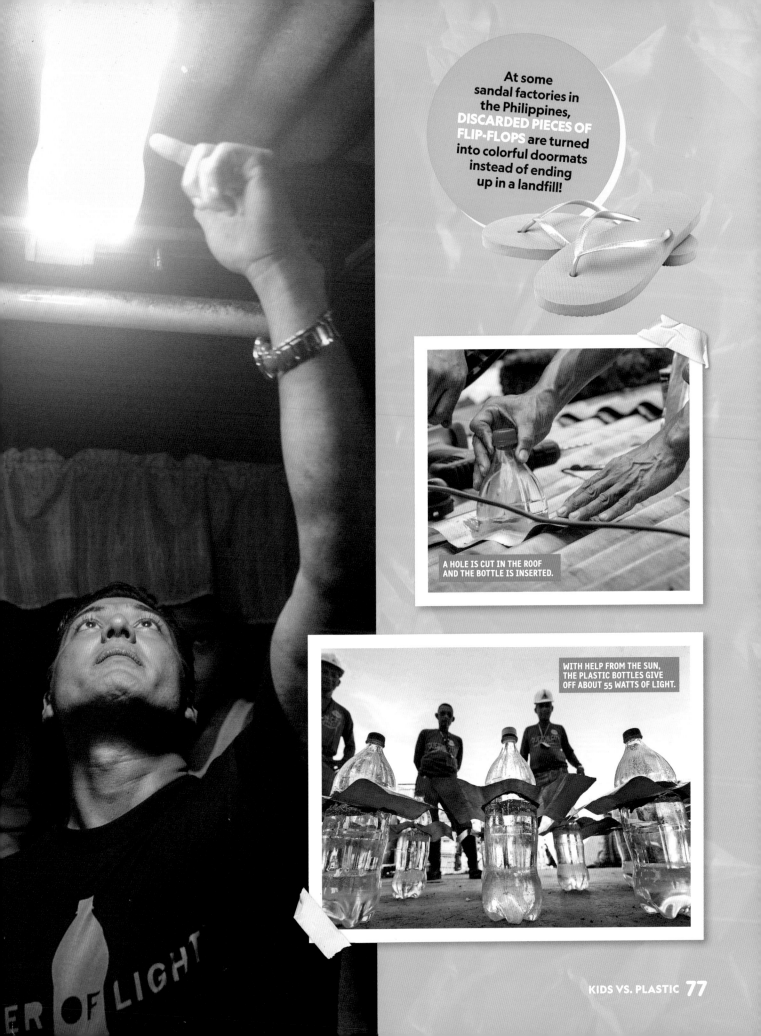

At some sandal factories in the Philippines, **DISCARDED PIECES OF FLIP-FLOPS** are turned into colorful doormats instead of ending up in a landfill!

A HOLE IS CUT IN THE ROOF AND THE BOTTLE IS INSERTED.

WITH HELP FROM THE SUN, THE PLASTIC BOTTLES GIVE OFF ABOUT 55 WATTS OF LIGHT.

# FROM TRASH TO ART

**DISCARDED PLASTIC IS GIVEN NEW LIFE—AND DELIVERS A MESSAGE ABOUT POLLUTION.**

To shed light on plastic's effect on marine animals, artists around the world are creating sculptures made from discarded single-use plastic or plastic fished from the sea.

Artists in England made a sculpture to show that plastic pollution is a whale of a problem. The "Bristol Whales" sculpture depicts a life-size humpback and blue whale swimming through an "ocean" of 70,000 plastic bottles, all of which were used and discarded during a local running race. The whales are made of locally harvested willow branches, and the bottles are made to look like waves and water droplets. The artists said they created the sculpture to show the amount of plastic that ends up in the world's oceans annually—which is the equivalent weight of 44,000 blue whales.

For an exhibit at Washington, D.C.'s Smithsonian National Zoo, 17 giant sculptures, from jellyfish to sharks, were made of plastic that had washed ashore along Pacific coastlines.

At San Francisco's Golden Gate National Recreation Area, the Monterey Bay Aquarium installed a life-size blue whale art installation made from discarded plastic. The artists noted that a blue whale can weigh about 300,000 pounds (136,078 kg)—the approximate weight of plastic that ends up in the ocean every nine minutes.

IN ENGLAND, A SCULPTURE OF A HUMPBACK WHALE SWIMS THROUGH AN "OCEAN" OF DISCARDED PLASTIC BOTTLES.

A JELLYFISH SCULPTURE MADE OF TRASH THAT WASHED ASHORE, ALSO PART OF THE SMITHSONIAN EXHIBIT, IS SHOWN HERE AT THE U.S. STATE DEPARTMENT, ANOTHER STOP ON ITS TOUR.

A SEAHORSE SCULPTURE MADE FROM DISCARDED PLASTIC AND OTHER TRASH WAS PART OF AN EXHIBIT OF "WASHED ASHORE" MATERIALS AT THE SMITHSONIAN NATIONAL ZOO IN WASHINGTON, D.C.

ARTISTS ASSEMBLE A SCULPTURE OF A WHALE MADE FROM DISCARDED PLASTIC AT SAN FRANCISCO'S GOLDEN GATE NATIONAL RECREATION AREA.

The **BLUE WHALE** is the **LARGEST ANIMAL** to ever live on Earth.

THE ARTISTS NOTED THAT EVERY NINE MINUTES, PLASTIC WEIGHING AS MUCH AS A BLUE WHALE ENTERS THE WORLD'S OCEANS.

# TURNING PLASTIC INTO FASHION

SHOES WERE EMBELLISHED USING SHARDS OF PLASTIC BOTTLES IN THE TRADITIONAL MOSAIC OF VALENCIA IN SPAIN.

## 178 PLASTIC BOTTLES WERE USED TO MAKE THIS DRESS!

### 178

**PLASTIC WATER BOTTLES:** 72 CLEAR, 53 GREEN, 26 BLUE, 26 PINK & 1 RED

**ROSA MONTESA WANTED TO MAKE A UNIQUE DRESS OUT OF RECYCLED OBJECTS FOR THE FALLAS**—a traditional celebration of the end of winter and the arrival of spring in her hometown of Valencia, Spain. But she knew she needed help, so she enlisted her 87-year-old mother to lend a hand with the sewing and her 17-year-old daughter volunteered to wear the final product at the celebration (although a family friend is seen wearing it here). After several months of designing and planning, Rosa got to work collecting recyclables, most of which were made from plastic. The bottoms of plastic bottles were glued to the fabric of the skirt of the dress, imitating a floral pattern. For the bodice, small pieces of plastic bottles were added to create a mosaic. "During the celebration of the Fallas, women wear traditional costumes made with expensive silk fabrics, embroidered with gold and silver threads," says Rosa. "Ours was a traditional dress made out of recycled materials."

Part of what makes plastic such a big problem, says Rosa, is its convenience. "Plastic is very cheap and easy to make into almost anything," Rosa says. "That is why we make an excessive use of it. The only way to stop the damage we're doing to the environment is by changing our consumption habits. Our goal was to show that trash can be a treasure, and we did it!"

# PAVING THE WAY
# WITH PLASTIC

## ONE COMPANY IS BUILDING ROADS WITH RECLAIMED PLASTIC.

**W**hat better way to drive home the point about reusing plastic than to turn plastic into something you can drive on? That was British engineer Toby McCartney's vision when he began building roads made partly of plastic bottles and bags.

Typically, roads are made up of 90 percent rock and sand and 10 percent bitumen, a sticky oil-based product. When McCartney was visiting India, he observed an inventive solution to filling potholes: People filled the holes with discarded plastic containers and melted them to form a seal. This started him thinking that perhaps plastic could be used not only to fix potholes, but also to make new roads. So, after some research and experimenting, he began grinding up discarded plastic and turning it into tiny pellets. McCartney uses these pellets to replace some of the bitumen—the key ingredient to sealing roads.

**MACREBUR**
*The plastic road company*

**THIS ROAD IS MADE FROM WASTE PLASTICS**
WWW.MACREBUR.COM

# STRONGER THAN TRADITIONAL ROADS

McCartney says the partially plastic roads—which have been built in parts of the United Kingdom, Canada, Australia, and New Zealand—are 60 percent stronger than traditional roads, and early tests show they may last up to three times longer.

British engineer Toby McCartney is building roads out of discarded plastic.

It might look like everyday asphalt, but this street is made with plastic.

**EVERY TON** of McCartney's special-recipe asphalt contains approximately **20,000 SINGLE-USE PLASTIC BOTTLES** or around **70,000 SINGLE-USE PLASTIC BAGS.**

## TO-GO TOTE

Help keep the Earth healthy by replacing some plastic items. Make a reusable bag to carry your lunch so you can ditch plastic bags and boxes, which take up landfill space.

### MATERIALS

- Old pair of jeans*
- Ruler
- Scissors
- Hot-glue gun
- Decorations like pom-poms, pins, lace, and patches

*Select a pair that you don't wear anymore—and have permission to cut up!

### TIP!

Pack a reusable water bottle and metal utensils in your new lunch bag.

### STEPS

**1** Measuring with the ruler, cut rectangles from the jeans in the following sizes: two pieces measuring 8 inches by 12 inches (20 cm by 30 cm) for the front and the back; two pieces measuring 4 inches by 12 inches (10 cm by 30 cm) for the two sides; one piece measuring 4 inches by 8 inches (10 cm by 20 cm) for the bottom.

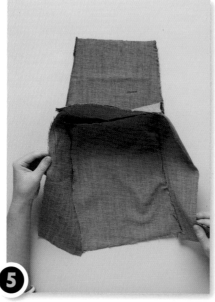

**5** Repeat steps 3 and 4 with all pieces along the bottom, then glue the side pieces to the front and back.

**6** Use more glue to seal any gaps along the bottom and edges. You should now have a sealed bag with four sides and a bottom. Next cut two strips of fabric from the jeans, each measuring about 6 inches (15 cm) long and 1 inch (2.5 cm) wide.

**2** Lay your rectangles on the table with the 4-by-8 piece in the middle, the 8-by-12 pieces on the top and bottom, and the 4-by-12 pieces on the sides.

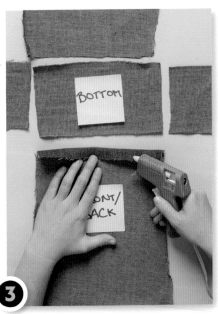

**3** Grab a parent and use the hot-glue gun to put a line of glue along the short edge of the front piece on the outside part of the jeans.

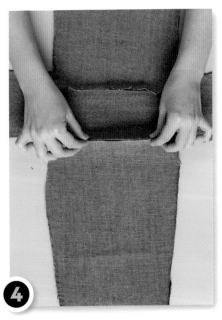

**4** Press the glue edge to the outside part of the bottom piece, carefully aligning the edges.

**7** Place a small dab of glue in the center of the front panel of the bag, about 3 inches (7.5 cm) from the top.

**8** Press one strip at this point, facing up and down. Repeat on the opposite side of the bag with the other strip.

**9** Decorate the outside of your lunch bag. Then to close it, roll the top of the bag down and tie the strips together.

CHECK OUT THIS CHAPTER TO DISCOVER HOW YOU CAN RECYCLE LIKE A PRO!

# CHAPTER 6

# THE END OF THE LINE: RECYCLE!

>> **IF YOU CAN'T REUSE IT OR REPURPOSE IT** into something else, there's only one thing left to do with plastic: Recycle it. Of all the plastic that has ever been produced, only 9 percent has been recycled. Why is that? Partly because recycling centers often don't accept all types of plastic, people aren't always clear about what types of plastic are recyclable in their communities, and some people don't make recycling plastic a priority. Learn how to make sure your plastic is on its way to being recycled into something new, rather than being sent to the landfill.

# THE LIFE CYCLE OF PLASTIC »

While tossing your plastic water bottle into the recycling bin is when you bid it adieu, it's just the first stage of its long journey to being turned into something new. Here's what happens after your plastic is hauled away:

**1** The contents of your curbside recycling bin are taken to a recycling center.

**7** The pellets are sold to companies to make new products, such as more plastic bottles, carpet, thread for clothes, and play equipment.

2. Workers at the center sort the recyclables by type, and the plastic is bundled up and often shipped to another facility for processing.

3. Plastic, including bottle caps, are ground into tiny pieces.

Plastic can be recycled two or three times before it's no longer of high enough quality to be used again.

4. Because they are two different types of plastic, the plastic pieces need to be sorted. They are put into water to be separated (the bits of plastic cap float and the bits of bottle sink).

5. The sorted plastic cap and bottle bits are washed and dried. Then each batch is heated into a liquid.

6. The liquid is stretched into thin strands, cooled, and chopped into small pellets.

# DECODE YOUR PLASTIC.

E ver notice those "chasing arrows" that form a triangle on the bottom of a plastic container or bottle? Inside that triangle is a number—a number that has more meaning than you might realize. The number—1 through 7—indicates the type of plastic a product is made from. Each plastic is composed of a different molecule or sets of molecules. Different types of molecules don't mix when they are processed, so these numbers are important to recycling companies. Some recycling companies only accept certain types of plastic. So, before sending something they don't accept, which might just get tossed, research another facility that might take it.

Check out the types of products that correspond to each number, and the new items they can be recycled into!

## NOT ALL RECYCLING FACILITIES ARE THE SAME.

Ask your parents to check with your local recycling center to see what can be recycled there and what can't. Often, there are separate facilities for discarded electronics, which is called e-waste. These items are partly made of plastic but may also contain hazardous materials that aren't safe to send to the landfill.

#1 **polyethylene terephthalate** including single-use water and soda bottles…

#2 **high-density polyethylene** including milk jugs…

#3 **polyvinyl chloride** including shampoo and cooking oil bottles…

#4 **low-density polyethylene** including thin plastic grocery bags and bread bags…

#5 **polypropylene** including yogurt lids…

#6 **polystyrene** including take-out plastic-foam containers…

#7 **other** including sunglasses and DVDs…

...can be **recycled** into fiber products, like carpets, and polyester fabrics, including fleece jackets.

...are **recycled** back into similar containers, or plastic lumber and traffic cones.

...are **recycled** into flooring and decks.

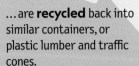

...are **recycled** into trash cans and floor tiles.

...are **often mixed with other resins** and made into items like road-marker reflectors.

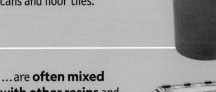

...often **cannot be recycled,** although some packing stores accept foam "peanuts" for reuse.

...often **can't be recycled** because they are a mix of different types of plastic, but they are sometimes made into plastic lumber.

**Plastic-foam packaging peanuts** may keep your breakables safe during shipping, but #6 plastic isn't safe for the environment—especially because the lightweight peanuts can easily escape garbage cans and trucks. Here's a simple alternative: unbuttered popcorn! It's surprisingly similar in structure to plastic-foam peanuts and can be composted upon delivery.

# TO-GO CUPS GO TO THE LANDFILL.

**To-go cups, such as the kind coffee shops sell, look and feel like paper,** but that doesn't mean they can be recycled like paper. In fact, most to-go cups can't be recycled at all. That's because the inside is lined with plastic to keep hot liquid from leaking out. Sixteen billion disposable coffee–style cups are tossed out every year. The good news: While companies work to finding ways to recycle the cups, there are plenty of cool reusable-cup options for you and your family.

# HIGH-TECH RECYCLING

## TRASH-SORTING ROBOTS KNOW HOW TO SPOT PLASTIC.

Sorting recyclables is messy and dangerous work. Recycling workers are more than twice as likely to be injured on the job. That may soon change, though. Artificial intelligence technology is coming soon to the trash-sorting scene.

Cameras and computers are being programmed to recognize plastic and then communicate with robots that move over a conveyor belt of recyclables. The plastic can be detected by shape, texture, and even logo. The robots then pick up the recyclables and toss them into bins. Early models have shown that the robots are as accurate as human workers and more than twice as fast. The hope is that the robots will reduce plastic heading to the landfill while keeping workers out of harm's way.

RECYCLABLES MOVE ALONG A CONVEYOR BELT FOR SORTING.

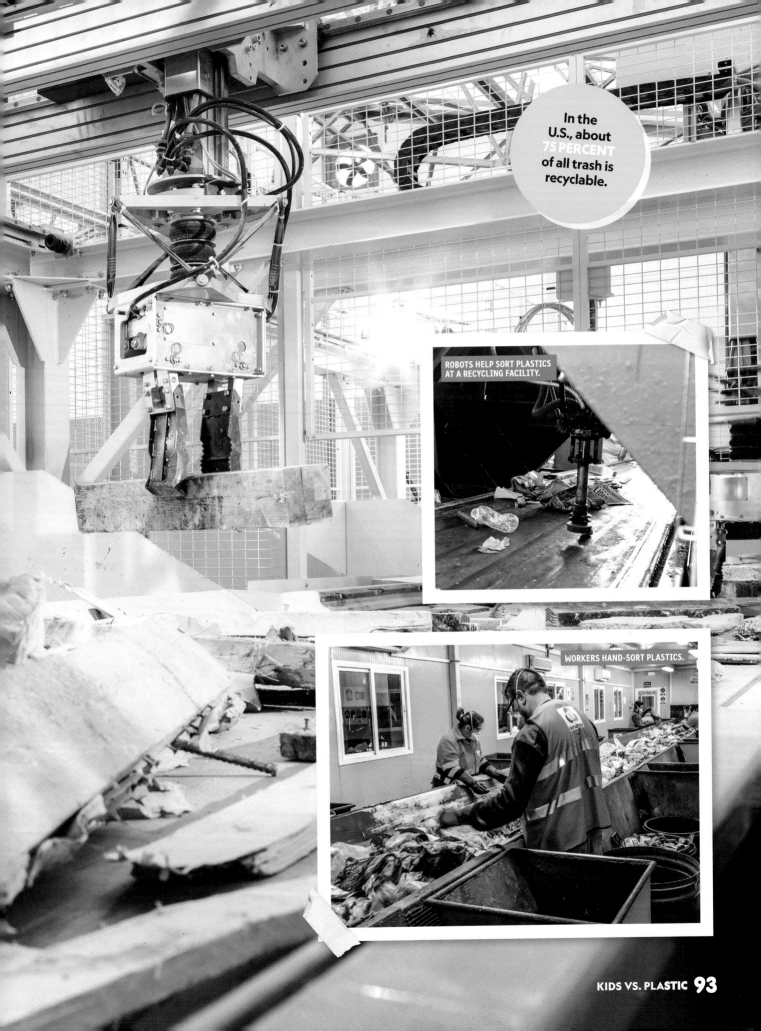

In the U.S., about **75 PERCENT** of all trash is recyclable.

ROBOTS HELP SORT PLASTICS AT A RECYCLING FACILITY.

WORKERS HAND-SORT PLASTICS.

# FROM BOTTLES TO BRACELETS

40CEAN FOUNDERS ANDREW COOPER (LEFT) AND ALEX SCHULZE

## Two surfers—and a dog!—pick up trash and turn it into jewelry.

Andrew Cooper and Alex Schulze, the founders of 4ocean, have a unique business model: If you buy one of their bracelets, they will collect and remove one pound (.45 kg) of plastic from the ocean. Their ocean cleanup sites are in the U.S., Bali, and Haiti, but their customers are worldwide. They told National Geographic via email about their ocean cleanups and about one particular employee especially keen on fetching plastic from the sea.

**Q: How did you get interested in cleaning up plastic from the ocean and beaches?**
**Andrew and Alex:** After college, we went on a surfing trip to Bali in search of big waves, but found beaches covered in garbage instead. We paddled through a devastating amount of plastic in the ocean and watched fishermen pull their boats through mounds of trash. When we returned home, we knew we had to do something about it.

**Q: Why did you decide to sell bracelets?**
**Andrew and Alex:** We wanted to sell a product that gave people around the world the opportunity to do their part to clean the ocean. The bracelet serves as a symbol of 4ocean's promise to pull a pound of trash from the ocean.

**Q: What are the bracelets made from?**
**Andrew and Alex:** The cord is made from recycled water bottles, and the beads are made from recycled glass bottles. The 4ocean charm that is attached to the bracelet is made from stainless steel.

4OCEAN BRACELETS ARE MADE FROM TRASH COLLECTED FROM THE OCEAN.

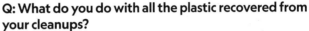
WORKERS SORT STRAWS FROM A PLASTIC-COLLECTION HAUL.

The BRACELET serves as a symbol of 4OCEAN'S PROMISE to pull a POUND (.45 kg) of TRASH FROM THE OCEAN for each one sold.

BALI BEFORE

A 4OCEAN CLEANUP SITE IN BALI

**Q: What do you do with all the plastic recovered from your cleanups?**
**Andrew and Alex:** It's sorted, compressed into bales, and either turned into raw materials that are used to create new products or stored for future use.

**Q: How much trash has 4ocean removed to date?**
**Andrew and Alex:** 4ocean has removed over seven million pounds [3.2 million kg] from the ocean and coastlines.

**Q: Your company has been cleaning up plastic for several years. What changes have you noticed as far as plastic in the ocean?**
**Andrew and Alex:** If we could clean up all the ocean plastic today, there would still be a problem tomorrow, because of the rate that plastic enters the ocean. With the continued use of plastic happening around the world every day, cleaning up ocean plastic is just part of the solution. Changing your habits is just as important. You can start by saying no to plastic straws when you are at a restaurant or bringing your own reusable bag to a store. These small changes make a big difference!

**Q: You have an amazing Labrador retriever named Lila who fetches plastic from beaches and even the water! What is Lila's role with 4ocean?**
**Andrew and Alex:** Lila represents that anyone can pick up plastic and keep the beaches and coastlines clean. If a dog can do it, so can you!

4OCEAN'S LABRADOR RETRIEVER, LILA

# HEADED
## OUT TO SEA

>> **O**nce plastic enters the ocean, it's on the move. Ocean currents send plastic to every corner of the globe—to remote islands in the South Pacific and even to the deepest points in the ocean. No one ever knew where all the plastic originally came from until National Geographic Explorer Jenna Jambeck worked with a team of scientists to figure it out. What they discovered was that a few countries are creating a lot of the plastic that ends up in the ocean. Half comes from China, the Philippines, Indonesia, and Vietnam. The United States also contributes a fair amount. In 2015, Jambeck and her colleagues published a study that broke down the total plastic waste produced per person in each of these countries, and it revealed how much of the plastic wasn't recycled. The study also showed how much of the plastic ended up in oceans. Here are the results.

NATIONAL GEOGRAPHIC EXPLORER JENNA JAMBECK HELPED FIGURE OUT WHERE ALL THE PLASTIC IN THE OCEAN WAS COMING FROM.

The **AMOUNT OF PLASTIC** that enters the oceans every year is equal to a volume of **FIVE GROCERY-SIZE BAGS** filled with plastic for **EVERY FOOT** of coastline in **THE WORLD.**

It is estimated that **BY 2025** the amount will increase to **10 GROCERY BAGS** per foot of coastline.

 Each bottle equals four pounds (4 lb/1.8 kg) of plastic waste. Data are per year.

## CHINA

Coastal population of 262.9 million generated 27.7% of global* mismanaged plastic waste

 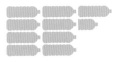  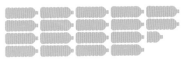 

97 lb of plastic waste produced per person

74 lb of which were mismanaged

As much as 30 lb of the plastic waste per person ended up in the ocean

## INDONESIA

Coastal population of 187.2 million generated 10.1% of global* mismanaged plastic waste

46 lb of plastic waste produced per person

38 lb of which were mismanaged

As much as 15 lb of the plastic waste per person ended up in the ocean

## PHILIPPINES

Coastal population of 83.4 million generated 5.9% of global* mismanaged plastic waste

 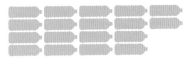 

60 lb of plastic waste produced per person

50 lb of which were mismanaged

As much as 20 lb of the plastic waste per person ended up in the ocean

## VIETNAM

Coastal population of 55.9 million generated 5.8% of global* mismanaged plastic waste

83 lb of plastic waste produced per person

72 lb of which were mismanaged

As much as 29 lb of the plastic waste per person ended up in the ocean

## U.S.A.

Coastal population of 112.9 million generated 0.9% of global* mismanaged plastic waste

270 lb of plastic waste produced per person

6 lb of which were mismanaged

As much as 2 lb of the plastic waste per person ended up in the ocean

Note: *Global refers to 192 countries whose aggregate population represents 93% of the world's population.

Source: Jenna Jambeck et al., *Science* (Feb. 13, 2015)

# IS THAT RECYCLABLE?

**TEST YOUR RECYCLING SMARTS!** Guess which of these items are fine to toss into a recycling bin and which are generally non-recyclable. Check the answers below to see if you are an expert recycler!

## 1 PLASTIC-FOAM TAKE-OUT CONTAINER

## 2 YOGURT CONTAINER

## 3 PLASTIC SUNGLASSES

**NOT ALL RECYCLING FACILITIES ARE THE SAME.** The thumbs-down products featured here aren't accepted at many recycling facilities because they are tricky to process, but you should check with your local recycler to see which types of plastic it accepts and which ones it doesn't. Also, some online research may reveal specific companies and groups accepting plastic products that are normally difficult to recycle, such as water filters or coffee pods.

# 4 PLASTIC SODA BOTTLE

# 5 TO-GO COFFEE CUP

# 6 MILK JUG

# 7 SHAMPOO BOTTLE

# 8 STRAWS

## Answers

👍 **Thumbs-up**

2. **Yogurt container** [Usually categorized as #5 plastic, you should be able to recycle these, as long as your recycling company accepts them.] 4. **Plastic soda bottle** [Usually categorized as #1 plastic, soda bottles are generally recyclable.] 6. **Milk jug** [Usually categorized as #2 plastic, milk jugs are generally recyclable.] 7. **Shampoo bottle** [Usually categorized as #3 plastic, you should be able to recycle these, as long as your recycling company accepts them.]

👎 **Thumbs-down**

1. **Plastic-foam take-out container** [Categorized as #6 plastic, foam is not accepted at most recycling facilities.] 3. **Plastic sunglasses** [Likely categorized as #7 plastic, sunglasses are often made from several types of plastic and generally aren't recyclable.] 5. **To-go coffee cup** [They look like paper, but to-go coffee cups have a plastic lining on the inside. The cups generally aren't recyclable.] 8. **Straws** [Most recycling companies are not equipped to recycle straws.]

# TRY THIS!

## Recycling Bin or Craft Store?

Rethink your recyclables to turn them into something creative and fun!

### Turn two large soda bottles ... into a jet pack.

### Turn juice bottles ... into a bottle garden.

Cut a juice bottle in half and fill it with soil. Plant flowers or vegetables and attach to a trellis or fence with wire.

Wrap two soda bottles in spare aluminum foil. (Ask your parents first, and don't forget, you can reuse the foil later!) Cut out felt or use colored tissue paper for flames and get ready to blast off.

## Turn a peanut butter jar ... into a bird feeder.

All done with your peanut butter? Don't toss it in the trash! Instead, sprinkle some bird seed around the inside so it sticks to the leftover peanut butter remaining in the jar, and then place it or hang it outside somewhere for the birds to find!

## Turn a water bottle ... into a piggy bank.

Use craft paper to turn a water bottle into a piggy bank. Use scissors to make a slot for coins.

## Turn a shampoo container ... into a pencil holder.

Creatively cut the top off of a shampoo bottle. Paint and personalize it by adding craft accessories such as pipe cleaners, decorative tape, pom-poms, and felt.

## Turn drinking straws ... into a vase.

Cut used plastic straws to size, then glue onto a used container.

RECYCLABLES IN MELBOURNE, AUSTRALIA, PILE UP AFTER A RECYCLING COMPANY DECLARED BANKRUPTCY. BECAUSE OTHER COMPANIES ARE UNABLE TO PROCESS THE MATERIALS, MUCH OF THE RECYCLABLE WASTE IS BEING SENT TO LANDFILLS.

# CHAPTER 7

# LOOKING AHEAD

>> ### WHAT'S THE SOLUTION TO PLASTIC POLLUTION?

And now for the big questions: Can we curb our plastic habit? Can we turn all the plastic waste into something useful? What do experts predict our future world will look like when it comes to plastic? Will there be an entirely new product that replaces plastic? Take a look at the ingenious ways people around the globe are combating our giant plastic problem and some innovative ideas they've come up with. With their brainpower and passion—and yours!—there's hope for the future health of our planet.

# YUM, PLASTIC!

## SCIENTISTS ACCIDENTALLY CREATED A MUTANT ENZYME THAT EATS PLASTIC!

One of the biggest problems with plastic is that it is slow—very slow—to biodegrade. A cardboard box takes two months to biodegrade. Plywood can take three years. Plastic can take hundreds of years. But scientists may have figured out a way to speed up that biodegrading process, thanks to a happy accident. In 2016, researchers at a Japanese recycling plant discovered a strain of bacteria that eats plastic—specifically PET, a common plastic used in making soda and water bottles. Then, while scientists in the U.K. and the U.S. were studying an enzyme in the bacteria, they accidentally created a "mutant enzyme" that can break down plastic in a few days! It normally takes PET hundreds of years to break down. Researchers don't think this is the solution to the heaps of plastic sitting in recycling centers around the world, but someday, it may play a part in the recycling process.

RESEARCHERS ARE STUDYING AN ENZYME IN ONE TYPE OF BACTERIA THAT CAN RAPIDLY BREAK DOWN PLASTIC.

# A MARINE ANIMAL THAT EATS AND POOPS PLASTIC

**The giant larvacean,** a four-inch (10-cm)-long type of plankton species found in the Pacific Ocean, surrounds itself in a translucent blob of mucus. The blob—called its house—allows it to take in water and other tiny animals to eat. And sometimes, it ingests microplastics. This is of interest to scientists studying ways to clean up this ocean hazard. Maybe these animals are the secret to cleaning up microplastic in the future?

CAN THIS PLANKTON HELP CLEAN UP MICROPLASTIC FROM THE OCEAN?

There is one problem: What goes in (that is, the microplastic) must come out—in the giant larvacean's poop. Further research has shown that the larvacean not only eats the plastic, it then poops it out, down at the ocean floor. Other animals then eat the poop, along with the larvacean's discarded mucus house. All of which means that while animals might be able to teach us a thing or two about cool, plastic-collecting systems, the plastic problem is still ours to solve.

TEEN SCIENCE FAIR WINNER ANGELINA ARORA TURNED SHRIMP SHELLS INTO A PLASTIC-LIKE PRODUCT.

Angelina's **SHRIMP-BASED PLASTIC** breaks down 1.5 million times **FASTER** than conventional plastic.

# SOMETHING FISHY ABOUT THIS "PLASTIC"

## AN AUSTRALIAN TEEN INVENTED A PLASTIC ALTERNATIVE THAT BREAKS DOWN IN A MONTH!

This science fair project puts exploding volcanoes to shame! Sixteen-year-old Angelina Arora from Sydney, Australia, was inspired to find an alternative to plastic after learning how many grocery bags are used only once and then thrown away. So, as part of a science project, she started looking into natural products similar in structure to plastic. It turns out, shrimp were just what she was fishing for.

Shrimp shells usually go to waste, but Angelina decided to grind some up into a powder and soak them to remove any minerals. Then she added a product called fibroin, a protein found in silkworm cocoons. Once the products were blended and dried, she pressed them into sheets that look a lot like plastic. The shrimp shell plastic is 90 percent as strong as the thin plastic used in disposable grocery bags. What's the big difference between Angelina's plastic and the kind used to make grocery bags? Hers breaks down in 33 days!

Angelina didn't come up with the shrimp-shell plastic overnight. There were trials and errors, and even an experiment involving banana peels. But when she noticed the similarities between shrimp shells and plastic, she knew she was on to something.

Her hard work and ingenuity paid off. Angelina won national and international awards—and even a scholarship to a university. Shrimp-based plastic hasn't hit the mainstream yet, but one day these food scraps may provide an alternative to single-use plastic.

THE SHRIMP-BASED PLASTIC BREAKS DOWN IN 33 DAYS.

# THE FUTURE IS SPARKLY.

## SCIENTISTS LOOK TO TREES FOR AN ECO-FRIENDLY ALTERNATIVE TO GLITTER.

**D**id you know glitter is a microplastic? Bummer! And because glitter is inherently tiny and used in some makeup, it can easily end up down the drain and in oceans. Luckily, scientists are finding alternatives to these microplastics—in trees! Some glitter is already being made in part from eucalyptus trees. To make this glitter, fibers from a tree are extracted and made into a film that looks and acts like plastic. The extract is metallized with a thin layer of aluminum and colored to give it its sparkle.

FRANCES SANSAO IS THE FOUNDER OF PURA, A BRAZILIAN COMPANY THAT MAKES BIODEGRADABLE GLITTER.

THIS GLITTER SPARKLES, BUT IT IS MADE FROM PLANTS, NOT PLASTIC.

# MOVE OVER, PLASTIC!

Sustainable glitter isn't the only eco-friendly alternative to plastic that is turning heads. Here are three more up-and-comers that you could be seeing more of in the future.

## ECO SIX-PACK BEVERAGE RINGS

Six-pack beverage rings have proved to be a major hazard for marine life, which can get caught up and trapped in them or mistake them for food. One company found a safer alternative: six-pack holders made from wheat and barley that look like paper. The material biodegrades quickly, and if an animal were to eat it, it wouldn't upset its digestive system.

## EDIBLE WATER BOTTLE

Here's an outside-the-bottle plastic solution: an edible water container. Sound like something from a sci-fi movie? Well, the future is here. Oohos are little round pouches of water you pop into your mouth. When you do, they turn into a gulp of water, with no waste to throw away. The pouches are created by dipping frozen balls of water into a tasteless algae mixture. The ice melts, but the algae membrane seals the water so it doesn't leak. To "eat" it, you can either pop it into your mouth, where the membrane instantly dissolves, or you can take a bite and sip the water out.

## BAMBOO TOOTHBRUSHES

Your dentist has probably told you that it's important to replace your toothbrush every three to four months so that you have nice fresh bristles to clean your pearly whites. Every time you do, though, you are throwing away plastic. What if your toothbrush handle were made from one of the fastest growing plants on Earth—bamboo? The bristles are usually still made from plastic, but all the rest of the tooth-brush is bamboo and can be composted.

# IMAGINING THE FUTURE OF PLASTIC

### With National Geographic Explorer Jenna Jambeck

National Geographic Explorer and University of Georgia associate professor Jenna Jambeck studies plastic pollution and has calculated how much plastic is washed into oceans.

**Q: If you could envision a perfect plan for the future when it comes to plastic, what would you like to see?**
**Jenna:** Plastic is really useful for durable things we want to last a long time, and for things like electronics and medical equipment. However, we use it too much for packaging and single-use items. To me, the ideal would be to be really thoughtful about where, when, and how we use plastic, and then to think through exactly how to recycle it when we're done using it—and design for that.

**Q: Do you think all the plastic in the oceans will be cleaned up anytime soon?**
**Jenna:** It is really hard to clean up the plastic in the ocean—most of it is the size of pencil erasers and smaller. A better solution would be cleaning it up on land and keeping it out of the ocean. And the best case is not having it leak into our environment in the first place.

**Q: Is the solution to plastic pollution in finding replacement materials to plastic or learning to do with less?**
**Jenna:** The solution is both of these. Waste reduction, especially in the United States and European Union, is important. The United States produces double or more waste per person than many other countries in the world. So we can do with less—less packaging and less single-use plastic. But not all packaging will go away, and there are other materials that can be used instead: paper, metal, and newer, truly biodegradable polymers.

VOLUNTEERS COLLECT TRASH DURING A BEACH CLEANUP.

The UNITED STATES produces double or more waste per person THAN MANY OTHER COUNTRIES in the world.

SCHOOLCHILDREN IN BALI, INDONESIA, CELEBRATE EARTH DAY BY CLEANING UP AN AREA OF MANGROVE FOREST NEAR A ROAD.

ONCE PRISTINE BEACHES ARE BECOMING POLLUTED WITH WASHED-ASHORE TRASH.

## Q: What can kids do to help solve the plastic pollution problem?

**Jenna:** Here are four big ways you can help:

- Start with your own backyard. What do you see on your school grounds? Log all the litter you see around your school. What did you find? Are there any certain items that can be removed from use that are either ending up in the environment or not really needed? Or are there nonplastic alternatives? After you know more about this issue, share it with teachers, friends, and family.

- Do community cleanups together, so you can see what is in your environment. Seeing what winds up as litter might inspire you to make different choices in the future.

- Investigate where your waste goes. Take a field trip to your local recycling facility or landfill. I'm sure what you find will be eye-opening.

- Realize that every choice you make, no matter how small, can make a difference. When you and all your classmates or peers around the world are making a similar choice, you will have a big global impact.

# BUILDING BLOCKS
## OF THE FUTURE

### A CITY MADE OF RECLAIMED PLASTIC? IT'S POSSIBLE.

**B**uildings are traditionally made out of wood, steel, and concrete. Given the mountains of plastic that have accumulated over the decades, though, can we add plastic to the list? One scientist thinks so.

Architect and National Geographic Emerging Explorer Arthur Huang invented the portable, solar-powered "Trashpresso," a machine that turns plastic waste into small tiles that can be used to build walls and floors. Here's how it works: Plastic waste is put into the machine's shredder, and the resulting flakes are washed. The flakes are then sent to a dryer and pressed into a mold. The molds are put into an oven to melt into tiles. The water used in the process is recycled back into the system, and the whole machine is powered by solar panels. Arthur says the aim is to create as little environmental impact in the tile-making process as possible.

The tiles have been used in the building of everything from a museum to a sporting goods store. Because the Trashpresso is portable, it can be taken to remote places, like the Tibetan Plateau, which suffers from issues of plastic waste just like more urbanized areas around the world.

NATIONAL GEOGRAPHIC EMERGING EXPLORER ARTHUR HUANG INVENTED A MACHINE THAT TURNS PLASTIC INTO BUILDING TILES.

MOLDED TILE MADE FROM PLASTIC

# TURNING POLLUTION INTO A PARK

recycledpark.com

Recycled park is the proposal to retrieve plastic litter from river and ports just before it reaches the sea. The plastics are recycled to give new value to the river. From the plastics we construct floating platforms for a new green environment floating park. Floating parks are a plus for the city and fulfill and ecological role in the river water.

**This Dutch city collected plastic from the river and turned it into a park—and habitat for animals.**

In Rotterdam, a city in the Netherlands, plastic from the river, which was once an eyesore and a danger to marine animals, is now transformed into a public space where people hang out and into a habitat for fish and birds. Sound like a city of the future? Well, there might be more projects like this one, based on its success.

Recycled Park is a floating park made entirely of recycled plastic collected from the river the park floats on. Specially designed watercraft scoop up plastic from the city's Nieuwe Maas River. The materials are then sorted and turned into building blocks used for a floating seating area for visitors to the park, as well as habitats for fish and marine birds. Park planners intend to expand the park as more plastic is collected and more building blocks are made.

# PLASTIC SMARTS

## 4 WAYS TO CURB PLASTIC AT SCHOOL

>> Reducing plastic shouldn't be a thing you just do at home. Take your plastic-fighting superpowers to the classroom! Here are four simple ways to cut down on plastic waste at school.

**1** **Shop for school supplies ...** at home. Before you go to the store to buy new supplies for the school year, first take inventory of what you already have. Can any of those binders from last year be reused? You likely have rulers, folders, and pens around the house. No need to buy more if you already have some, right? Shop at home to save money and plastic!

**2** **Use wooden, not plastic, pencils.** As long as your teacher says it's OK, go the old-school route and use good old yellow pencils. Once the plastic ones wear out, they go into the trash. The wooden ones just become shavings!

**4** **Use reusable containers** for your sandwich and snacks, or try a tiffin lunch box. The metal lunchbox, widely used in South Asia, comes with two, three, or four compartments that nest neatly, with no need for any plastic storage containers.

**3** **Repurpose your markers.** Crayola has a program called ColorCycle in which schools in the contiguous United States and parts of Canada can mail in their markers to be melted down and made into new products. Schools just need to register online, fill up a cardboard box of any brand of 100 used markers, print a shipping label, and send the markers on to a new life!

# Certificate of Heroism

**This hereby recognizes**

.......................................................

.......................................................

as a **PLANET PROTECTOR**, pledging to help save the world by decreasing the use of straws, water bottles, and other single-use plastic items.

**GARY E. KNELL**
Chief Executive Officer
National Geographic Partners

**NATIONAL GEOGRAPHIC KiDS**

# NATIONAL GEOGRAPHIC GEOCHALLENGE WINNERS

>> **MEET THE KIDS WHO CAME UP WITH SOLUTIONS TO TACKLE PLASTIC POLLUTION.**

In this book, we've seen that kids can come up with some pretty smart ideas to help tackle problems surrounding plastic—from writing scientific papers about the effect of golf balls on the ocean to inventing a new plastic-like product from shrimp shells. National Geographic set out to hear more bright ideas from young people by hosting the GeoChallenge. Kids in grades five through eight across the United States were eligible to enter the contest, and were asked to develop a creative solution for the real-world problem of plastic pollution.

Students formed teams of four to six people and used skills such as teamwork, research, innovation, critical thinking, and persuasive communication while creating their projects. The top teams advanced to the regional and then national level. The finals were held in Washington, D.C. Check out the winning idea!

MEMBERS OF THE "NAVIGATORS," A TEAM OF FIFTH GRADERS FROM FLUSHING, NEW YORK, WHO WERE WINNERS OF THE 2019 NATIONAL GEOGRAPHIC GEOCHALLENGE. THE STUDENTS DESIGNED A FILTRATION DEVICE THAT WOULD FIT ON THE FRONT OF A BOAT AND FILTER MICROPLASTICS OUT OF THE HUDSON RIVER.

## POM-POM PUFFS

Help keep the Earth healthy by skipping single-use plastic items. Decorate your next party with paper pom-pom balls instead of balloons.

Why? Balloons released into the air or left outside can end up in the ocean, where they might entangle animals.

### ⊻ MATERIALS

- 8 sheets of equal-size tissue paper (Bigger tissue paper will make bigger pom-poms.)
- 1 craft pipe cleaner
- Scissors
- String (optional)

## TIP!

**Instead of releasing a balloon to make a wish, blow out candles.**

### ⊻ STEPS

**1** Stack 8 sheets of tissue paper together. (You can use the same color or mix it up.) Fold the tissue paper back and forth in 1-inch (2.5-cm) sections like an accordion. Press each fold.

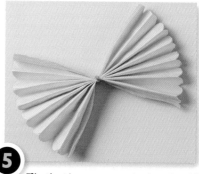

**5** Flip the tissue-paper stack on its side.

**6** Separate each layer of tissue paper one at a time.

**4** Cut both ends of the tissue-paper stack into rounded, pointed, or frilly shapes.

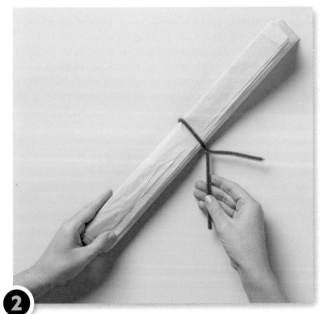

**2** Wrap the pipe cleaner around the center of the folded tissue-paper stack, then twist the pipe cleaner to secure it.

**3** Trim the pipe cleaner with scissors, then wrap the end of the pipe cleaner around itself so the wire doesn't poke out.

**7** Pull the layers up and toward the center.

**8** To hang your pom-pom, tie a piece of string to the center of the pipe cleaner.

# 25 MORE WAYS YOU CAN SAVE THE OCEAN FROM PLASTIC

Trying to reduce the amount of plastic that you use can feel overwhelming. It's OK if you can't do everything—just getting started is the important part.

Hurray! You are officially an expert on all things plastic. And, as a Planet Protector, you know that plastic causes big problems when it makes its way into the ocean. There's a lot you can do to help! As you take what you've learned into the world, use these tips to reduce the amount of single-use plastic you use, as well as take care of the plastic you already have. Together, we can protect ocean animals and keep Earth clean! Onward!

## PROJECT PLASTIC

You can't avoid plastic all the time, so here's how to keep the stuff you have from harming the environment.

**1** Don't put garbage on top of an overflowing trash can. It can easily blow away and wind up in waterways.

**2** Swap plastic toys with your friends instead of asking for brand-new things.

**3** Take old electronics with plastic pieces to a recycling station or back to an electronics store instead of putting it in the regular trash. (Make sure the store accepts the item first.)

**4** Give single-use plastic a new job, like using newspaper sleeves to pick up pet poo.

**5** Ask your fave pizza place to **LEAVE OUT THE LITTLE PLASTIC TABLE** in your delivery box.

**6** Carry a bag with a **REUSABLE WATER BOTTLE,** cup, and utensils so you can skip the plastic stuff wherever you go.

**7** Make a sandwich out of **FRESH BREAD FROM A BAKERY** instead of packaged grocery store bread.

**8** Order your **ICE-CREAM SCOOPS** served in a cone instead of a cup. No plastic spoon needed!

**9** Give your friends **PLASTIC-FREE GIFTS** like homemade treats, sidewalk chalk, or movie tickets.

**10** Get **SQUEAKY CLEAN** with a bar of soap instead of bottled liquid wash.

**11** Use junk mail and old newspapers instead of bubbled plastic to **PAD BREAKABLE STUFF.**

**12** **GET CRAFTY** with crayons and colored pencils instead of markers.

**13** **TO FRESHEN UP A STINKY ROOM,** place a bar of soap in your laundry hamper and spritz your shoes and sheets with white vinegar instead of using plastic plug-ins or spray bottles.

**14** Make sure your plastic **BEACH TOYS** don't get washed away by the waves.

**15** Instead of packaged treats, snack on **STOVETOP POPCORN,** nuts, trail mix, cereal, and candies bought from the bulk-foods section of your grocery store (and gathered in reusable bags).

## MAKE NOISE

If you *really* want to make an impact, ask businesses and governments to get involved, too.

**16** Does your favorite restaurant or ice-cream shop offer plastic straws and spoons? Ask an adult to help you reach out to these businesses about swapping the items for paper or plant-based options. Learn how online. natgeokids.com /KidsVsPlastic

**17** Report plastic litter to your local government. By tracking the items people see most often, the government might change laws about trash.

**18** Send your used plastic food wrappers back to the company with a letter asking them to change the packaging.

**19** Ask your teacher to help you create a plastic project in your classroom. Start by recording all the plastic your class throws away in one week, then talk about ways to reduce what you see.

**20** Send a letter, postcard, or drawing to local and high-level representatives or even the president asking them to do something about plastic pollution.

## RECYCLE RIGHT

Experts estimate that only about 9 percent of the world's plastic gets recycled. Follow these steps to make sure your local recycling plant can accept the plastic in your bin.

**21** Visit your city's website to learn what your local recycling plant can take.

**22** Clean and dry your recyclables. (If items are covered in food and grease, they might be sent to the landfill instead.)

**23** Don't forget the lids for containers like soda bottles, shampoo bottles, and mouthwash containers; the lids should get recycled, too.

**24** Put all of your items into the recycling bin separately, not in bags or containers.

**25** Plastic grocery bags, bubbled plastic, and Styrofoam can gum up the sorting machines, so keep these items out of the recycling bin. Instead, take Styrofoam packing peanuts to a mailing center to be reused, and bring the rest to the grocery store to be recycled separately.

# INDEX

# INDEX

# PHOTO CREDITS

**Cover** (bag), Poprugin Aleksey/Shutterstock; (UP RT), Sergi Garcia Fernandez/Biosphoto; (utensils), Rob Hyrons/Shutterstock; (toothbrush), BalancePhoto/Shutterstock; (balloons), weerapat1003/Adobe Stock; (LO RT), Anton Starikov/Shutterstock; (straws), photka/Adobe Stock; (straws), Olha/Adobe Stock; (net), Kletr/Shutterstock; (bottle), Picsfive/Shutterstock; **spine** (utensils), Rob Hyrons/Shutterstock; **back cover** (net), Kletr/Shutterstock; (balloons), weerapat1003/Adobe Stock; (CTR RT), photka/Shutterstock; (LO RT), Petlyaroman/Dreamstime; (LO LE), vitals/Adobe Stock; (UP LE), Photodisc

**Front Matter:** 1, Brooke Becker/Adobe Stock; 2, Mohamed Abdulraheem/Shutterstock; 3 (UP RT), Sergi Garcia Fernandez/Biosphoto; 3 (LO RT), Anton Starikov/Shutterstock; 3 (LO LE), vitals/Adobe Stock; 4 (UP CTR), KPPWC/Adobe Stock; 4 (UP RT), Tatsiana/Adobe Stock; 4 (LO LE), Clearwater Marine Aquarium; 5 (UP LE), Jay Directo/AFP via Getty Images; 5, (UP RT), Washed Ashore: Art to Save the Sea; 5 (LO), 4ocean; 6 (UP), Photodisc; 6 (earbuds), Noppadol_1/Shutterstock; 6 (CTR), Thongden Studio/Shutterstock; 6 (LO LE), Heike Brauer/Shutterstock; 6 (LO RT), Photodisc; 6 (frog), akids.photo.graphy/Shutterstock; 7 (UP LE), Trong Nguyen/Shutterstock; 7 (UP RT), J. Helgason/Shutterstock; 7 (RT), Petlyaroman/Dreamstime

**Chapter 1:** 8–9, Africa Studio/Adobe Stock; 10 (LE), nikitos77/Adobe Stock; 10 (RT), Rob Wilson/Shutterstock; 11 (UP), Nerthuz/Alamy Stock Photo; 11 (RT), Michael Sheehan/Dreamstime; 11 (LO), RomanYa/Shutterstock; 11 (LE), David Fleetham/Nature Picture Library; 12–13, trialartinf/Adobe Stock; 13 (UP RT), imageegami/Adobe Stock; 13 (LO RT), vladimirzuev/Adobe Stock; 13 (LO CTR), Cavan/Alamy Stock Photo; 13 (LO LE), Science & Society Picture Library/Getty Images; 13 (CTR LE), Bettmann/Getty Images; 13 (UP LE), boyzzzzz/Adobe Stock; 14–15, zodebala/Getty Images; 15 (UP), Jacobs Stock Photography Ltd/Getty Images; 15 (CTR), SeeCee/Shutterstock; 15 (LE), Norbert Pouchain/EyeEm/Getty Images; 16–17, Gus Tello; 17 (INSET), fotofabrika/Adobe Stock; 18 (UP LE), JRP Studio/Adobe Stock; 18 (UP RT), Sara Tabin for Seven Days; 18 (LO), Danita Delimont/Alamy Stock Photo; 19 (LE), jipen/Adobe Stock; 19 (RT), Ruslan Grumble/Adobe Stock; 19 (bag), aopsan/Getty Images; 19 (blue), lindaoqian/Adobe Stock; 19 (green), eurobanks/Adobe Stock; 20 (LE), Zonda/Shutterstock; 20 (RT), Willee Cole/Adobe Stock; 21 (UP LE), Fred Dufour/AFP via Getty Images/Getty Images; 21 (splash), Ljubisa Sujica/Dreamstime; 21 (bottle), pixarno/Adobe Stock; 21 (faucet), Juri/Adobe Stock; 21 (pink), Joyce Vincent/Shutterstock; 21 (LO RT), Patti McConville/Alamy Stock Photo; 21 (LO LE), GlobalStock/Getty Images; 22–23, Simon Potter/Getty Images

**Chapter 2:** 24, Flip Nicklin/Minden Pictures; 26 (LE), bimka/Shutterstock; 26 (LO), Tunatura/Adobe Stock; 27 (UP), Stockagogo by Barhorst/Shutterstock; 27 (CTR RT), Scisetti Alfio/Adobe Stock; 27 (LO RT), I'm friday/Shutterstock; 27 (LO LE), lunamarina/Shutterstock; 27 (CTR), Kiev.Victor/Shutterstock; 28–29, Studio One-One/Getty Images; 28, Sergi Garcia Fernandez/Biosphoto; 29 (UP), Rebecca Drobis/National Geographic Image Collection; 29 (LO), Africa Studio/Shutterstock; 29 (LE), Steve Trewhella/FLPA/Minden Pictures; 30–31 (LE), nalinratphi/Shutterstock; 30 (CTR), Kim Reinick/Shutterstock; 30 (RT), Emily Brauner/Ocean Conservancy; 31 (UP RT), Mushy/Adobe Stock; 31 (LO RT), EasternLightcraft/Getty Images; 31 (LO LE), SeDmi/Shutterstock; 31 (plate),

Dmytro Sandratskyi/Adobe Stock; 31 (cups), wolfelarry/Adobe Stock; 31 (lid), Anton Starikov/Shutterstock; 31 (bag), Chones/Shutterstock; 32–33, Luis Javier Sandoval Alvarado/Alamy Stock Photo; 33 (UP), Clearwater Marine Aquarium; 33 (CTR), Clearwater Marine Aquarium; 33 (LO), Clearwater Marine Aquarium; 33, NG Maps; 34–35, Steve De Neef/National Geographic Image Collection; 34 (LE), Pete Atkinson/Getty Images; 34 (RT), Aflo/Shutterstock; 35 (LE), NG Maps; 35 (RT), photka/Shutterstock; 36 (UP), Neil Tolbert; 36 (LO), Allison Jarrell; 37 (UP), Daimon Hickman; 37 (LO), photka/Shutterstock; 38, Thomas P. Peschak/National Geographic Image Collection; 39 (CTR RT), Velvetfish/Getty Images; 39 (LO RT), Jak Wonderly; 39 (LO CTR), Richard Herrmann/Minden Pictures; 39 (LO LE), Magnus Larsson/Getty Images

**Chapter 3:** 40–41, untungsubagyo/Shutterstock; 42 (CTR), mandritoiu/Adobe Stock; 42 (CTR LE), jcfotografo/Adobe Stock; 42 (LO LE), Coprid/Adobe Stock; 42 (LO RT), SeanPavonePhoto/Adobe Stock; 43 (UP LE), picsfive/Adobe Stock; 43 (UP CTR), Tiger Images/Shutterstock; 43 (LO RT), Mariyana M/Shutterstock; 43 (money), ppart/Shutterstock; 43 (CTR LE), saiko3p/Adobe Stock; 44 (LO LE), Benjamin Clapp/Adobe Stock; 44 (LO CTR), sunstock/Getty Images; 44 (CTR), koosen/Adobe Stock; 44 (LO RT), Mr. Music/Adobe Stock; 45 (tumbler), New Africa/Adobe Stock; 45 (LO RT), KPPWCAdobe Stock; 45 (bag), Chones/Shutterstock; 45 (metal), AlenKadr/Adobe Stock; 45 (LO LE), jummie/Adobe Stock; 45 (UP CTR), vitals/Adobe Stock; 46–47, jfbenning/Getty Images; 46, Caroline Field Photography; 47 (UP), Paul Nicholls Photography; 47 (CTR), Vitaliy Myasnikov/Adobe Stock; 47 (LO), Stocksy/Adobe Stock; 48 (UP & LO), Alex Weber; 49 (UP LE), The Plastic Pick-Up; 49 (UP RT), Robert Beck/Sports Illustrated via Getty Images/Getty Images; 49 (CTR), The Plastic Pick-Up; 49 (LO), Robert Beck/Sports Illustrated via Getty Images; 50–51, Artyom Knyaz/Adobe Stock; 50, Jiri Hera/Adobe Stock; 51 (UP RT), Scisetti Alfio/Adobe Stock; 51 (CTR, LO RT & LO LE), Courtesy Two Farmers; 51 (bags), Courtesy Two Farmers; 52 (UP RT), Rawpixel/Shutterstock; 52 (LO RT), isaac74/Adobe Stock; 52 (ketchup), Moving Moment/Adobe Stock; 52 (mayo), Moving Moment/Adobe Stock; 52 (CTR LE), xamtiw/Adobe Stock; 53 (UP LE), Photo_SS/Shutterstock; 53 (UP RT), jummie/Adobe Stock; 53 (LO RT), dkidpix/Adobe Stock; 53 (LO LE), SDI Productions/Getty Images; 54 (buildings), Johnny Adolphson/Shutterstock; 54 (owl), Eric Isselee/Shutterstock; 54 (giraffe), Eric Isselee/Shutterstock; 54 (cheetah), Maros Bauer/Shutterstock; 54 (octopus), zhengzaishuru/Shutterstock; 54 (eagle), Adam Jones/Getty Images; 54 (lions), jez_bennett/Getty Images; 55 (bottles), Africa Studio/Shutterstock; 55 (box), M. Unal Ozmen/Shutterstock; 55 (rings), You Touch Pix of EuToch/Shutterstock; 55 (food), baibaz/Getty Images; 55 (clock), stockshoppe/Shutterstock; 55 (balloon), Bo Valentino/Shutterstock; 55 (bag), photka/Shutterstock; 55 (dolphin), Tory Kallman/Shutterstock; 55 (duck), Martin Fowler/Shutterstock; 55 (seal), Accent Alaska/Alamy Stock Photo; 55 (shark), Toby C./Getty Images; 55 (turtle), Luis Javier Sandoval Alvarado/Alamy Stock Photo

**Chapter 4:** 56–57, Westend61/Getty Images; 58 (LE), Anna Hoychuk/Adobe Stock; 58 (CTR), Janis Smits/Adobe Stock; 58 (RT), misskaterina/Adobe Stock; 59 (UP CTR), Salena Stinchcombe/Shutterstock; 59 (wrap), nndanko/Adobe Stock; 59 (CTR RT), Loren Jon Photographer/Shutterstock; 59 (LO RT), kuarmungadd/Adobe Stock; 59 (LO CTR), Elnur/Dreamstime; 59 (cone), unpict/Adobe

Stock; 59 (LO LE), homydesign/Adobe Stock; 60–61, fotobieshutterb/Adobe Stock; 60, Petrychenko Anton/Shutterstock; 61 (UP), Tatsiana/Adobe Stock; 61 (CTR, rope & box), Green Toys, Inc.; 61 (LE), ricka_kinamoto/Adobe Stock; 62 (UP), Hannamariah/Shutterstock; 62 (LO LE), Adisa/Shutterstock; 62 (LO CTR), Sergey Novikov/Adobe Stock; 62 (LO RT), arztsamui/Adobe Stock; 63 (UP CTR), vimax001/Adobe Stock; 63 (RT), JPC-PROD/Shutterstock; 63 (LO CTR), Lenscap Photography/Shutterstock; 63 (LO LE), Ryan Davren; 64 (LE), Nina Dewji; 64 (LO), Evan Lorne/Shutterstock; 65 (UP), Aleksei Potov/Adobe Stock; 65 (green/blue), Lightfield Studios/Adobe Stock; 65 (brown), fotomaximum/Adobe Stock; 65 (red), picsfive/Adobe Stock; 65 (pink), fotomaximum/Adobe Stock; 65 (caps), Chones/Shutterstock; 65 (wrappers), JpegPhotographer/Shutterstock; 65 (tape), Picsfive/Shutterstock; 65 (battery), fotomaximum/Adobe Stock; 65 (floss), Lightfield Studios/Adobe Stock; 65 (yellow), Lightfield Studios/Adobe Stock; 65 (jar), AlenKadr/Adobe Stock; 65 (caps), Chones/Shutterstock; 65 (blue), fotomaximum/Adobe Stock; 65 (string), citramonP/Adobe Stock; 65 (wrappers), JpegPhotographer/Shutterstock; 66–67, jfunk/Adobe Stock; 66 (UP), fahrwasser/Adobe Stock; 66 (CTR), Liliya Trott/Adobe Stock; 66 (LO), Vladimir Sukhachev/Shutterstock; 67 (UP), Rachael Hamm Plett; 67 (LO), B.G. Photography/Adobe Stock; 68–69, Masezdromaderi/Dreamstime

**Chapter 5:** 70–71, Washed Ashore: Art to Save the Sea; 72–73, NOAA/NMFS/Pacific Islands Fisheries Science Center Blog; 72, EasternLightcraft/Getty Images; 73 (1), Solent News/Shutterstock; 73 (2), Dhiraj Singh/Bloomberg via Getty Images; 73 (3), Danny Chan/Alamy Live News; 73 (4), Libby Welch/Alamy Stock Photo; 73 (5), 33333/Shutterstock; 73 (6), gogoiso/Shutterstock; 73 (7), Nikolai Sorokin/Dreamstime; 73 (8), Dave M. Benett/Dave Benett/Getty Images for BRITA; 73 (9), Reuters/Michaela Rehle; 73 (10), mimo/Shutterstock; 74 (UP LE), oqba/Adobe Stock; 74 (LO LE), Jessica Babcock; 74 (CTR RT), yvon52/Shutterstock; 74 (LO RT), Lisa White/A Twist of Sumerset; 75 (CTR RT), Roninphotography/Dreamstime; 75 (LO RT), Anders Bertelsen; 75 (CTR LO), Lindsay Eidahl/MyCreativeDays; 75 (CTR), Lindsay Eidahl/MyCreativeDays; 75 (zebra), Adobe Stock; 75 (giraffe), goofygolf/Shutterstock; 76–77, Jay Directo/AFP via Getty Images; 76, Hyrma/Adobe Stock; 77 (UP), Studio KIVI/Adobe Stock; 77 (CTR), Jay Directo/AFP via Getty Images; 77 (LO), Dondi Tawatao/Getty Images; 78–79, AP Photo/Eric Risberg; 78 (UP), Ben Gillett/Nature Picture Library; 78 (LO RT & LO LE), Washed Ashore: Art to Save the Sea; 79, AP Photo/Eric Risberg; 80–81 (ALL), Eva Ripoll Photo Design; 82–83, Courtesy MacRebur; 83 (UP), Geoff Pugh/Shutterstock; 83 (CTR), Courtesy MacRebur; 83 (bag), Chones/Shutterstock; 83 (LO LE), AlenKadr/Shutterstock; 84 (ALL), Becky Hale/NG Studio; 84 (LO LE), suradech14/Adobe Stock; 84 (LO CTR), Sviatlana/Adobe Stock

**Chapter 6:** 86–87, Rawpixel/Adobe Stock; 88 (UP), Mariyana M/Shutterstock; 88 (1), Rtimages/Dreamstime; 89 (2), Pavel/Adobe Stock; 89 (3), digitalstock/Adobe Stock; 89 (4), Universal History Archive/Shutterstock; 89 (5), wittaya photo/Shutterstock; 89 (6), Philip Rozenski/Shutterstock; 88 (7), Rosmarie Wirz/Getty Images; 89 (CTR), warloka79/Adobe Stock; 90 (1), Yellow Cat/Shutterstock; 90 (2), bestv/Shutterstock; 90 (3), Rose Carson/Shutterstock; 90 (4), Ratikova/Shutterstock; 90 (5), Anton Starikov/Shutterstock; 90 (6), jipatafoto89/Shutterstock; 90 (7up), Alexey Filatov/Shutterstock; 90 (7lo), Bell nipon/Shutterstock; 91 (1),

nys/Adobe Stock; 91 (2), Nikolayn/Dreamstime; 91 (3), davidmariuz/Adobe Stock; 91 (4), BlureArt/Adobe Stock; 91 (5), Ton Bangkeaw/Shutterstock; 91 (6), eskay lim/Adobe Stock; 91 (7), frog/Adobe Stock; 91 (UP RT), Melica/Shutterstock; 91 (LO RT), Mariusz Blach/Adobe Stock; 92–93, Courtesy of ZenRobotics; 92, Francois Lo Presti/AFP via Getty Images; 93 (CTR), Francois Lo Presti/AFP via Getty Images; 93 (LO), Charly Morlock/Shutterstock; 94–95 (ALL), 4ocean; 96–97, alphaspirit/Adobe Stock; 96, University of Georgia Marketing & Communications. All rights reserved.; 98 (LE), smartik1988/Adobe Stock; 98 (RT), Coprid/Adobe Stock; 98 (LO), Javier brosch/Adobe Stock; 99 (UP LE), picsfive/Adobe Stock; 99 (UP CTR), bestv/Shutterstock; 99 (UP RT), Mariusz Blach/Adobe Stock; 99 (CTR RT), Daisy Daisy/Adobe Stock; 99 (bottle), vovan/Adobe Stock; 99 (LO LE), Michael Flippo/Adobe Stock; 100 (UP), Coprid/Adobe Stock; 100 (CTR RT), Reimphoto/Getty Images; 100 (LO LE), Jan Woitas/dpa-Zentralbild/ZB/dpa/Alamy Live News; 100 (CTR LE), Steve Cukrov/Shutterstock; 101 (UP LE), phloen/Shutterstock; 101 (UP CTR), Sloot/Getty Images; 101 (UP RT), Vsevolodizotov/Shutterstock; 101 (CTR RT), Rachael Hamm Plett; 101 (LO CTR), Cheattha/Adobe Stock; 101 (LO LE), koya979/Shutterstock; 101 (bank), Dorling Kindersley Ltd/Alamy Stock Photo; 101 (CTR LE), Mariyana M/Shutterstock

**Chapter 7:** 102–103, Jason South/The Age via Getty Images; 104–105, Peak Sailor/Shutterstock; 104, Dr_Microbe/Getty Images; 105 (UP), Jonathan Blair/National Geographic Image Collection; 105 (LO), Bluefin/Adobe Stock; 106–107, Louise Kennerley/Fairfax Media via Getty Images; 107, Eldred Lim/Shutterstock; 108–109, Carl De Souza/AFP via Getty Image; 108, Carl De Souza/AFP via Getty Images; 109 (UP), Pavel Timofeev/Adobe Stock; 109 (CTR RT), E6PR SAPI de CV; 109 (CTR LE), Notpla; 109 (LO), Rostislav Sedlacek/Adobe Stock; 110–111, Cheattha/Adobe Stock; 110 (UP), AP Photo/Seth Borenstein; 110 (LO), Seanglerd/Adobe Stock; 111 (UP), Pande Putu Hadi Wiguna/Shutterstock; 111, PhotographyByMK/Adobe Stock; 112–113, MINIWIZ; 112 (CTR), Chris Tzou/Bloomberg via Getty Images; 112 (LO), MINIWIZ; 112 (LO), MINIWIZ; 113, Cover Images/Newscom; 114–115, lamaip/Adobe Stock; 114 (LE), zaikina/Adobe Stock; 114 (RT), Africa Studio/Shutterstock; 115 (UP), UlrikaArt/Adobe Stock; 115 (LO), Budimir Jevtic/Adobe Stock; 116 (Earth), Somchai Som/Shutterstock; 116 (trash bag), Scisetti Alfio/Adobe Stock; 116 (cup), vitals/Adobe Stock; 116 (bag), Chones/Shutterstock; 116 (bluewater), Yellow Cat/Shutterstock; 116 (clearwater), AlenKadr/Shutterstock; 116 (green), SeDmi/Shutterstock; 116 (rings), You Touch Pix of EuToch/Shutterstock; 116 (plate), siraphol/Adobe Stock; 116 (bottle), Ekkaphan Chimpalee/Shutterstock; 116 (cutlery), Coprid/Adobe Stock; 116 (blue & lime), apimook/Adobe Stock; 116 (water), Mariyana M/Shutterstock; 116 (straws), Tiger Images/Shutterstock; 117 (UP), Adam Steckley; 117 (CTR), Mark Thiessen/NG Staff; 117 (LO), Adam Steckley; 118–119 (ALL), Becky Hale/NG Studio; 118 (LE), Sylvia Wendorf/Dreamstime; 120 (6), Lalandrew/Shutterstock; 120 (9), hopshomemade/Getty Images; 120 (8), pixelliebe/Shutterstock; 120 (5), Dima Sikorsky/Shutterstock; 121 (11), Vorobyeva/Shutterstock; 121 (13), Ivonne Wierink/Shutterstock; 121 (14), nafterphoto/Shutterstock; 121 (15), William Scott/Alamy Stock Photo; 121 (LO RT), photka/Shutterstock

**End matter:** 128, Brooke Becker/Adobe Stock

**FOR THE YOUNG PLANET PROTECTORS RYAN, MILO, AND ALEX.
YOUR WORK AND DEDICATION TO CLEANING UP AND REDUCING
PLASTIC POLLUTION IS TRULY AN INSPIRATION. —JB**

Since 1888, the National Geographic Society has funded more than 12,000 research, exploration, and preservation projects around the world. The Society receives funds from National Geographic Partners, LLC, funded in part by your purchase. A portion of the proceeds from this book supports this vital work. To learn more, visit natgeo.com/info.

For more information, visit nationalgeographic.com, call 1-877-873-6846, or write to the following address:

National Geographic Partners
1145 17th Street N.W.
Washington, DC 20036-4688 U.S.A.

For librarians and teachers: nationalgeographic.com/books/librarians-and-educators

More for kids from National Geographic: natgeokids.com

*National Geographic Kids* magazine inspires children to explore their world with fun yet educational articles on animals, science, nature, and more. Using fresh storytelling and amazing photography, *Nat Geo Kids* shows kids ages 6 to 14 the fascinating truth about the world—and why they should care.
**kids.nationalgeographic.com/subscribe**

For rights or permissions inquiries, please contact National Geographic Books Subsidiary Rights: bookrights@natgeo.com

The publisher would like to acknowledge everyone who helped make this book possible: Ariane Szu-Tu, editor; Lisa M. Gerry, project editor; Amanda Larsen, art director; Sarah Mock and Shannon Hibberd, photo editors; Joan Gossett, production editor; Anne LeongSon and Gus Tello, design production assistants; Jennifer Kelly Geddes, fact-checker; and the tireless explorers, researchers, and scientists of the National Geographic Society.

Select pages from this book are adapted from the following stories in *National Geographic Kids* magazine:

Pages 32–33, adapted from: Allyson Shaw, "Sea Turtle Rescue," April 2019, pp. 18–19; pp. 46–47, adapted from: Allyson Shaw, "Mr. Trash Wheel," April 2019, p. 15; pp. 54–55, adapted from: Kay Boatner, "Personality Quiz," April 2019, pp. 12–13; pp. 118–119, adapted from: Ella Schwartz, "Make This to Avoid That," April 2019, p. 33; pp. 120–121, adapted from: Allyson Shaw, "35 Ways You Can Save the Ocean From Plastic," April 2019, pp. 24–25.

Designed by Rachael Hamm Plett, Lauren Loran, Sanjida Rashid, Gus Tello, Anne LeongSon, and Shannon Pallatta

Trade paperback ISBN: 978-1-4263-3910-3
Reinforced library binding ISBN: 978-1-4263-3911-0

Printed in Malaysia
20/QRM/1